A DREAM CATCHER'S
JOURNAL ...

Capturing The Mood

By: Annala d'
©2021

I AM,

_____,

AND THIS IS MY DREAM JOURNAL.
THE DREAMS I ENTER INTO
THIS JOURNAL PROVIDES A PATH
THAT LEADS TO MY GOOD HEALTH,
SUCCESS AND PROSPERITY.

Introduction

Our conscious mind is at rest when we dream. When we sleep, our subconscious mind activates and so begins our journey into a different reality. The world of dreams can be exhilarating, frightening, encouraging, and enlightening, but just as often, they present things we do not understand. After waking it is only a short time before our consciousness reclaims our mind and quickly, we forget most of our dreams. There may be a few that stay with us for days or even weeks, but with time, these dreams lose their importance because our conscious mind distorts their original significance.

Many people discount their dreams, especially those dream memories they think of as weird or unreal. However, every dream you have has a significant meaning. Never dismiss your dream. ***The Book of Numbers, Chapter 12, Verse 6 tells us that the Universal Creator speaks to us through dreams.***

I suggest you keep a recorder and a journal by your bed. As soon as you wake up, do not jump up. Open your eyes slowly and allow your conscious mind to let your dream appear, and your dream will present itself to you. Record your dream immediately. It's alright to electronically record your dreams, but also write them down. When you write down your dreams, they become more tangible and lasting in your life, and writing them down provides you a roadmap.

Dreams allow our Creator and Spiritual Guides to communicate through your subconscious. When you consciously understand your dreams, you can chart a more prosperous and productive path.

If you lack the discipline to record your dreams, you will discover that you will most likely not remember your dreams at all. The Creator knocks at your door through dreams, but the door will not remain open unless you consciously will it. Think of this: Would you continue and try to guide someone if they did not respect the assistance you were providing? Would you continue providing directions for someone who did not take the time to write down the information? The revelation of dreams is available but it's up to you to reach for them.

Peace, Love, and Prosperity,

What Were You Taught About Dream Interpretation?

Were you taught that having your dreams interpreted is the work of a devil? I am here to let you know that is not true. Do you know that dream interpretation dates back to 3000-4000 B.C? Dream interpretation was practiced long ago, and clay tablets were used to document this fact. In fact, the Bible teaches that God communicates through dreams. I don't know about you, but I have always been fascinated with the possibility of insight through dreams for myself as well as for others. Providing dream interpretations has allowed me and countless others to maneuver through many paths in my life.

Brief History of Dream Interpretation:

Some primal society members were unable to distinguish between the dream world and the waking world. Or they could simply choose not to make the distinction. They saw that the dream world was not only an extension of reality, but that it was a more powerful world.

Do you know that in the Greek and Roman eras, dreams were seen in a religious context? They were believed to be direct messages from the gods or from the dead. The people of that time look to their dreams for solutions on what to do or what course of action to take. They believed dreams forewarned and predicted the future. Special shrines were even built where people could go to sleep in hopes that a message would be passed to them through their dreams. Their belief in the power of a dream was so strong that it even dictated the actions of political and military leaders. In fact, dream interpreters even accompanied military leaders into battle to help with war strategy.

Greek philosopher Aristotle believed that dreams were a result of physiological functions. Through dreams diseases could be predicted and diagnosed.

Alfred Adler (1870 -1937) believed that dreams are an important tool to mastering control over our waking lives. They are problem-solving devices. Dreams need to be brought to the conscious and interpreted so that better understanding can be shed on your problems.

During the Hellenistic period, the main focus of dreams was centered around its ability to heal. Temples, called Asclepions, were built around the healing power of dreams. It was believed that sick people who slept in these temples would be sent cures through their dreams. Dream interpreters even aided the medicine men in their medical diagnosis. It was believed that dreams offered a vital clue for healers to find what was wrong with the dreamer.

In Egypt, priests also acted as dream interpreters. The Egyptians recorded their dreams in hieroglyphics. People with particularly vivid and significant dreams were believed to be blessed and were considered special. People who had the power to interpret dreams were looked up to and seen as divinely gifted. This is evidenced in the Bible story of Joseph. Joseph was known as one who had the ability to interpret dreams. This is not the only story about dreams in the bible. The bible has over seven hundred references to dreams.

https://shifttothereal.com/idreammagus/

Dreams can be seen as actual places that your spirit and soul sojourns to. The Chinese believed that the soul leaves the body to go into this world. However, if they should be suddenly awakened, their soul may fail to return to the body. For this reason, some Chinese, even today, are wary of alarm clocks. Some Native American tribes and Mexican civilizations share this same notion of a distinct dream dimension. They believed that their ancestors live in their dreams and take on non-human forms like plants. They see dreams as a way of visiting and having contact with their ancestors. Dreams also help to point out their mission or role in life.

Remember when I mentioned that some of us were taught that dreams were the words of a devil? In the vulnerable sleep state, the devil was believed to fill the mind of humans with poisonous thoughts. He did his dirty work through dreams, attempting to mislead us down a sinful path.

In the early 19th century, dreams were dismissed as stemming from anxiety, a household noise, or even indigestion. Hence there was really no meaning to it. Later on in the 19th century, Sigmund Freud revived the importance of dreams and the need for dream interpretation. He revolutionized the study of dreams.

Tracing back to these ancient cultures, people have always been inclined to believe in a deeper meaning to their dreams. They naturally sought out the help and guidance of dream interpreters. There is absolutely nothing evil or unnatural about people wanting to understand their own psyche.

Dream Moods

Daydreams

Daydreaming is classified as a level of consciousness between sleep and wakefulness. Studies show that you have the tendency to daydream an average of 70-120 minutes a day. It occurs during waking hours when you let your imagination carry you away. As your mind begins to wander and your level of awareness decreases, you lose yourself in your imagined scenario and fantasy.

False Awakening Dreams

Have you ever thought you have woke up and gone about your daily morning routine: getting up, brushing your teeth, eating breakfast and going to work, only to wake up "again" and realize that what just happened was a dream? That sensation is referred to as a false awakening.

Lucid Dreams

Lucid dreams occur when you realize you are dreaming. "Wait a second. This is only a dream!" Most dreamers wake themselves up once they realize that they are dreaming. Other dreamers have cultivated the skill to remain in the lucid state of dreaming. They become an active participant in their own dreams, making decisions in their dreams and influencing the dream's outcome without awakening.

Nightmares

A nightmare is a disturbing dream that causes you to wake up feeling anxious and frightened. Nightmares may be a response to real life trauma and situations. These types of nightmares fall under a special category called Post-traumatic Stress Nightmare (PSN). Nightmares may also occur because you have ignored or refused to accept a particular life situation. Research shows that most people who have regular nightmares have a family history of psychiatric problems, are involved in a rocky relationship or have had bad drug experiences. These people may have also contemplated suicide. Nightmares are an indication of a fear that needs to be acknowledged and confronted. It is a way for the subconscious to wake up and take notice. "Pay attention!"

Recurring Dreams

Recurring dreams repeat themselves with little variation in story or theme. These dreams may be positive, but most often they are nightmarish in content. Dreams may recur because a conflict depicted in the dream remains unresolved or ignored. Once you find a resolution to the problem, your recurring dreams will cease.

Healing Dreams

Healing dreams serve as messages for the dreamer in regard to their health. The Ancient Greeks called these dreams "prodromic". Many dream experts believe that dreams can help in avoiding potential health problems, even healing when you are ill or when you are grieving. Research shows that asthma and migraine sufferers have certain types of dreams before an attack. The body is able to communicate to the mind through dreams. The dreams can "tell" you that something is not quite right with the body even before any physical symptoms show up. Dreams of this nature may be telling the dreamer that he or she needs to go to the dentist or doctor. If you can understand the language of dreams they will act as an invaluable early warning system. They can help inform, advise and heal.

Prophetic Dreams

Prophetic dreams, also referred to as precognitive or psychic dreams, are dreams that seemingly foretell the future. One rational theory to explain this phenomenon is that your dreaming mind is able to piece together bits of information and observation that you may normally overlook or that you do not seriously consider. In other words, your unconscious mind knows what is coming before you piece it together in your conscious mind.

Signal Dreams

Signal dreams show you how to solve problems or make decisions in your waking life.

Epic Dreams

Epic dreams (also referred to as Great Dreams, Cosmic Dreams or Numinous Dreams) are so huge, so compelling, and so vivid that you cannot ignore them. The details of such dreams remain with you for years, as if you just dreamt it last night. These dreams possess much beauty and contain many archetypal symbology. When you wake up from such a dream, you feel that you have discovered something profound or amazing about yourself or about the world. It feels like a life-changing experience.

Progressive Dreams

Progressive dreams occur when you have a sequence of dreams that continue over a period of nights. The dream continues where you left off the previous night. Such dreams are problem-solving dreams and help to explore different options and various approaches to a problem, situation, or relationship.

Mutual Dreams

Mutual dreams are when two people have the same dream. Mutual dreams may be planned, meaning that two people actively work toward achieving one dream scenario or goal. It is a way to improve communication and build trust. Mutual dreams can also be spontaneous. You find out that a friend, a significant other, faraway relative, or someone has had the same dream on the same night as you. Not much study has gone into the phenomenon of mutual dreams, but there is a very strong bond that exists between these two people.

Dream Statistics:

1. One-third of your life is spent sleeping.

2. In an average lifetime, you would have spent a total of about six years of it dreaming. That is more than 2,100 days spent in a different realm!

3. Dreams have been here as long as mankind. Back in the Roman Era, profound and significant dreams were submitted to the Senate for analysis and interpretation.

4. Most healthy people have dreams. Some people don't believe they dream at night when in fact they just don't remember.

5. Dreams are indispensable. A lack of dream activity may imply some protein deficiency or a personality disorder.

6. On average, you can dream anywhere from one to two hours every night. Moreover, you can have four to seven dreams in one night.

7. Blind people do dream. Whether visual images appear in their dreams depend on whether they were blind at birth or became blind later in life. But vision is not the only sense that constitutes a dream. Sound, tactility, and smell become hypersensitive for the blind and their dreams are based on these senses.

8. Five minutes after the end of the dream, half the content is forgotten. After ten minutes, 90% is lost.

9. The word dream stems from the Middle English word, dreme which means "joy" and "music".

   https://shifttothereal.com/idreammagus/

10. Men tend to dream more about other men, while women dream equally about men and women.

11. Studies have shown that your brain waves are more active during dreaming than when awake.

12. Dreamers who are awakened right after REM sleep, can recall their dreams more vividly than those who slept through the night until morning.

13. Physiologically speaking, researchers found that during dreaming REM sleep, males experience erections and females experience increased vaginal blood flow, regardless of the content of the dream. In fact, "wet dreams" may not necessarily coincide with overtly sexual dream content.

14. People who are in the process of giving up smoking tend to have longer and more intense dreams.

15. Toddlers do not dream about themselves. They do not appear in their own dreams until the age of 3 or 4.

16. If you are snoring, then you cannot be dreaming.

17. Nightmares are common in children, typically beginning at around age 3 and occurring up to age 7-9.

18. In a poll, 68% of Americans have experienced Deja Vu in their dreams, occurring more often in females than males.

19. Around 3% of adults suffer from sleep apnea. This treatable condition leads to unexplained tiredness and inefficiency.

20. According to a research study, the most common setting for dreams is your own house.

21. It is very normal for males to experience an erection during the REM stage of sleep, even when they are not dreaming anything of a sexual nature.

22. The original meaning of the word «nightmare" was a female spirit who besets people at night while they sleep.

23. 23. In dreams, negative emotions tend to occur twice as often as pleasant feelings. Fear and anxiety are the most expressed emotions in dreams, followed by anger and sadness.

Why Should You Remember Your Dreams?

1. Your dreaming mind has access to vital information that is not readily available to you when you are awake. Your dreams serve as a window to your subconscious and reveal your secret desires and feelings.

2. In remembering your dreams, you gain increased knowledge, self-awareness and self-healing. Dreams are an extension of how you perceive yourself. They may be a source of inspiration, wisdom, joy, imagination, and overall improved psychological health.

3. Learning to recall your dreams help you become a more assertive, confident and stronger person. By remembering your dreams, you are expressing and confronting your feelings.

4. Dreams help guide you through difficult decisions, relationship issues, health concerns, career questions or any life struggle you may be experiencing.

5. Remembering your dreams helps you come to terms with stressful aspects of your lives.

6. You will learn more about yourself, your aspirations, and your desires through your dreams.

https://shifttothereal.com/idreammagus/

Affirm this statement before you sleep each night to assist in remembering your dreams:

My dreams come easily to me; I remember them quickly and clearly. I receive impressionable dreams and awaken to record them. I am grateful for the guidance of my dreams and the memories they provide to me. I am joyfully awakened by a Higher Power after my dream so that I can capture it. I appreciate all my dream impressions and gratefully receive them as insight and awaken to record them. I am thankful for my dreams.

Capturing Your Dream Mood

Date: _____ (Enter the date of your dream.)

1. Name the dream: _____ *(This name will typically be the theme or idea of the dream)*

2. How did you feel? _____ *(Afraid, happy, lost, confused, happy, angry, etc.)*

3. Describe the theme *(What was happening, i.e., on the beach, fighting, running, at a party, Day or night, sunny, raining, etc).*

_____

_____

_____

_____

_____

4. List every symbol *(Sofa, water, pool, shoe, dirt, car, truck, dog, mom, dad, sister, etc.)*

A._____   B._____

C._____   D._____

E._____   F._____

G._____   H._____

5. Describe the dream in detail, including its conclusion *(List every color and number that you remember)*

_____

_____

_____

_____

_____

6. Name and describe the individuals in your dream. *(If you do not know the person, state their role in your dream.)*

Their role in the dream	Who are they to you?
A. _____	_____
B. _____	_____
C. _____	_____
D. _____	_____

7. Describe any project(s) you are currently working on?

_____

_____

_____

_____

_____

8. Briefly describe something you encountered the day before you had this dream.

_____

_____

_____

_____

_____

9. What did you have on your mind before falling asleep on the night you had this dream?

_____

_____

_____

_____

_____

https://shifttothereal.com/idreammagus/

Date: _____ (Enter the date of your dream.)

1. Name the dream: _____ *(This name will typically be the theme or idea of the dream)*

2. How did you feel? _____ *(Afraid, happy, lost, confused, happy, angry, etc.)*

3. Describe the theme *(What was happening, i.e., on the beach, fighting, running, at a party, Day or night, sunny, raining, etc).*

_____

_____

_____

_____

_____

4. List every symbol *(Sofa, water, pool, shoe, dirt, car, truck, dog, mom, dad, sister, etc.)*

A._____   B._____

C._____   D._____

E._____   F._____

G._____   H._____

5. Describe the dream in detail, including its conclusion *(List every color and number that you remember)*

_____

_____

_____

_____

_____

6. Name and describe the individuals in your dream. *(If you do not know the person, state their role in your dream.)*

Their role in the dream   Who are they to you?

A. _____   _____

B. _____   _____

C. _____   _____

D. _____   _____

7. Describe any project(s) you are currently working on?

_____

_____

_____

_____

_____

8. Briefly describe something you encountered the day before you had this dream.

_____

_____

_____

_____

_____

9. What did you have on your mind before falling asleep on the night you had this dream?

_____

_____

_____

_____

_____

Date: _____ (Enter the date of your dream.)

1. Name the dream: _____ *(This name will typically be the theme or idea of the dream)*

2. How did you feel? _____ *(Afraid, happy, lost, confused, happy, angry, etc.)*

3. Describe the theme *(What was happening, i.e., on the beach, fighting, running, at a party, Day or night, sunny, raining, etc).*

_____

_____

_____

_____

_____

4. List every symbol *(Sofa, water, pool, shoe, dirt, car, truck, dog, mom, dad, sister, etc.)*

A._____   B._____

C._____   D._____

E._____   F._____

G._____   H._____

5. Describe the dream in detail, including its conclusion *(List every color and number that you remember)*

_____

_____

_____

_____

_____

6. Name and describe the individuals in your dream. *(If you do not know the person, state their role in your dream.)*

Their role in the dream   Who are they to you?

A. _____   _____

B. _____   _____

C. _____   _____

D. _____   _____

7. Describe any project(s) you are currently working on?

_____

_____

_____

_____

_____

8. Briefly describe something you encountered the day before you had this dream.

_____

_____

_____

_____

_____

9. What did you have on your mind before falling asleep on the night you had this dream?

_____

_____

_____

_____

_____

https://shifttothereal.com/idreammagus/

Date: _____ (Enter the date of your dream.)

1. Name the dream: _____ *(This name will typically be the theme or idea of the dream)*

2. How did you feel? _____ *(Afraid, happy, lost, confused, happy, angry, etc.)*

3. Describe the theme *(What was happening, i.e., on the beach, fighting, running, at a party, Day or night, sunny, raining, etc).*

_____

_____

_____

_____

_____

4. List every symbol *(Sofa, water, pool, shoe, dirt, car, truck, dog, mom, dad, sister, etc.)*

A._____   B._____

C._____   D._____

E._____   F._____

G._____   H._____

5. Describe the dream in detail, including its conclusion *(List every color and number that you remember)*

_____

_____

_____

_____

_____

6. Name and describe the individuals in your dream. *(If you do not know the person, state their role in your dream.)*

       Their role in the dream   Who are they to you?

A. _____   _____

B. _____   _____

C. _____   _____

D. _____   _____

7. Describe any project(s) you are currently working on?

_____

_____

_____

_____

_____

8. Briefly describe something you encountered the day before you had this dream.

_____

_____

_____

_____

_____

9. What did you have on your mind before falling asleep on the night you had this dream?

_____

_____

_____

_____

_____

       https://shifttothereal.com/idreammagus/

Date: _____ (Enter the date of your dream.)

1. Name the dream: _____ (*This name will typically be the theme or idea of the dream*)

2. How did you feel? _____ (*Afraid, happy, lost, confused, happy, angry, etc.*)

3. Describe the theme (*What was happening, i.e., on the beach, fighting, running, at a party, Day or night, sunny, raining, etc*).

_____

_____

_____

_____

_____

_____

4. List every symbol (*Sofa, water, pool, shoe, dirt, car, truck, dog, mom, dad, sister, etc.*)

A._____   B._____

C._____   D._____

E._____   F._____

G._____   H._____

5. Describe the dream in detail, including its conclusion (*List every color and number that you remember*)

_____

_____

_____

_____

_____

6. Name and describe the individuals in your dream. *(If you do not know the person, state their role in your dream.)*

Their role in the dream · · · · · · · · · · · · · · · Who are they to you?

A. _____ · · · · · · · · · · _____

B. _____ · · · · · · · · · · _____

C. _____ · · · · · · · · · · _____

D. _____ · · · · · · · · · · _____

7. Describe any project(s) you are currently working on?

_____

_____

_____

_____

_____

8. Briefly describe something you encountered the day before you had this dream.

_____

_____

_____

_____

_____

9. What did you have on your mind before falling asleep on the night you had this dream?

_____

_____

_____

_____

_____

Date: _____ (Enter the date of your dream.)

1. Name the dream: _____ *(This name will typically be the theme or idea of the dream)*

2. How did you feel? _____ *(Afraid, happy, lost, confused, happy, angry, etc.)*

3. Describe the theme *(What was happening, i.e., on the beach, fighting, running, at a party, Day or night, sunny, raining, etc).*

_____

_____

_____

_____

_____

4. List every symbol *(Sofa, water, pool, shoe, dirt, car, truck, dog, mom, dad, sister, etc.)*

A._____   B._____

C._____   D._____

E._____   F._____

G._____   H._____

5. Describe the dream in detail, including its conclusion *(List every color and number that you remember)*

_____

_____

_____

_____

_____

6. Name and describe the individuals in your dream. *(If you do not know the person, state their role in your dream.)*

        Their role in the dream   Who are they to you?

A. _____   _____

B. _____   _____

C. _____   _____

D. _____   _____

7. Describe any project(s) you are currently working on?

_____

_____

_____

_____

_____

8. Briefly describe something you encountered the day before you had this dream.

_____

_____

_____

_____

_____

9. What did you have on your mind before falling asleep on the night you had this dream?

_____

_____

_____

_____

_____

Date: _____ (Enter the date of your dream.)

1. Name the dream: _____ *(This name will typically be the theme or idea of the dream)*

2. How did you feel? _____ *(Afraid, happy, lost, confused, happy, angry, etc.)*

3. Describe the theme *(What was happening, i.e., on the beach, fighting, running, at a party, Day or night, sunny, raining, etc).*

_____

_____

_____

_____

_____

4. List every symbol *(Sofa, water, pool, shoe, dirt, car, truck, dog, mom, dad, sister, etc.)*

A._____   B._____

C._____   D._____

E._____   F._____

G._____   H._____

5. Describe the dream in detail, including its conclusion *(List every color and number that you remember)*

_____

_____

_____

_____

_____

6. Name and describe the individuals in your dream. *(If you do not know the person, state their role in your dream.)*

Their role in the dream   Who are they to you?

A. _____   _____

B. _____   _____

C. _____   _____

D. _____   _____

7. Describe any project(s) you are currently working on?

_____

_____

_____

_____

_____

8. Briefly describe something you encountered the day before you had this dream.

_____

_____

_____

_____

_____

9. What did you have on your mind before falling asleep on the night you had this dream?

_____

_____

_____

_____

_____

Date: _____ (Enter the date of your dream.)

1. Name the dream: _____ *(This name will typically be the theme or idea of the dream)*

2. How did you feel? _____ *(Afraid, happy, lost, confused, happy, angry, etc.)*

3. Describe the theme *(What was happening, i.e., on the beach, fighting, running, at a party, Day or night, sunny, raining, etc).*

_____

_____

_____

_____

_____

4. List every symbol *(Sofa, water, pool, shoe, dirt, car, truck, dog, mom, dad, sister, etc.)*

A._____   B._____

C._____   D._____

E._____   F._____

G._____   H._____

5. Describe the dream in detail, including its conclusion *(List every color and number that you remember)*

_____

_____

_____

_____

_____

6. Name and describe the individuals in your dream. *(If you do not know the person, state their role in your dream.)*

Their role in the dream   Who are they to you?

A. _____   _____

B. _____   _____

C. _____   _____

D. _____   _____

7. Describe any project(s) you are currently working on?

_____

_____

_____

_____

_____

8. Briefly describe something you encountered the day before you had this dream.

_____

_____

_____

_____

_____

9. What did you have on your mind before falling asleep on the night you had this dream?

_____

_____

_____

_____

_____

Date: _____ (Enter the date of your dream.)

1. Name the dream: _____ *(This name will typically be the theme or idea of the dream)*

2. How did you feel? _____ *(Afraid, happy, lost, confused, happy, angry, etc.)*

3. Describe the theme *(What was happening, i.e., on the beach, fighting, running, at a party, Day or night, sunny, raining, etc).*

_____

_____

_____

_____

_____

4. List every symbol *(Sofa, water, pool, shoe, dirt, car, truck, dog, mom, dad, sister, etc.)*

A._____   B._____

C._____   D._____

E._____   F._____

G._____   H._____

5. Describe the dream in detail, including its conclusion *(List every color and number that you remember)*

_____

_____

_____

_____

_____

6. Name and describe the individuals in your dream. *(If you do not know the person, state their role in your dream.)*

Their role in the dream   Who are they to you?

A. _____   _____

B. _____   _____

C. _____   _____

D. _____   _____

7. Describe any project(s) you are currently working on?

_____

_____

_____

_____

_____

8. Briefly describe something you encountered the day before you had this dream.

_____

_____

_____

_____

_____

9. What did you have on your mind before falling asleep on the night you had this dream?

_____

_____

_____

_____

_____

Date: _____ (Enter the date of your dream.)

1. Name the dream: _____ *(This name will typically be the theme or idea of the dream)*

2. How did you feel? _____ *(Afraid, happy, lost, confused, happy, angry, etc.)*

3. Describe the theme *(What was happening, i.e., on the beach, fighting, running, at a party, Day or night, sunny, raining, etc).*

_____

_____

_____

_____

_____

4. List every symbol *(Sofa, water, pool, shoe, dirt, car, truck, dog, mom, dad, sister, etc.)*

A._____   B._____

C._____   D._____

E._____   F._____

G._____   H._____

5. Describe the dream in detail, including its conclusion *(List every color and number that you remember)*

_____

_____

_____

_____

_____

6. Name and describe the individuals in your dream. *(If you do not know the person, state their role in your dream.)*

Their role in the dream   Who are they to you?

A. _____   _____

B. _____   _____

C. _____   _____

D. _____   _____

7. Describe any project(s) you are currently working on?

_____

_____

_____

_____

_____

8. Briefly describe something you encountered the day before you had this dream.

_____

_____

_____

_____

_____

9. What did you have on your mind before falling asleep on the night you had this dream?

_____

_____

_____

_____

_____

https://shifttothereal.com/idreammagus/

Date: _____ (Enter the date of your dream.)

1. Name the dream: _____ *(This name will typically be the theme or idea of the dream)*

2. How did you feel? _____ *(Afraid, happy, lost, confused, happy, angry, etc.)*

3. Describe the theme *(What was happening, i.e., on the beach, fighting, running, at a party, Day or night, sunny, raining, etc).*

_____

_____

_____

_____

_____

4. List every symbol *(Sofa, water, pool, shoe, dirt, car, truck, dog, mom, dad, sister, etc.)*

   A._____   B._____

   C._____   D._____

   E._____   F._____

   G._____   H._____

5. Describe the dream in detail, including its conclusion *(List every color and number that you remember)*

_____

_____

_____

_____

_____

6. Name and describe the individuals in your dream. *(If you do not know the person, state their role in your dream.)*

Their role in the dream   Who are they to you?

A. _____   _____

B. _____   _____

C. _____   _____

D. _____   _____

7. Describe any project(s) you are currently working on?

_____

_____

_____

_____

_____

8. Briefly describe something you encountered the day before you had this dream.

_____

_____

_____

_____

_____

9. What did you have on your mind before falling asleep on the night you had this dream?

_____

_____

_____

_____

_____

https://shifttothereal.com/idreammagus/

Date: _____ (Enter the date of your dream.)

1. Name the dream: _____ *(This name will typically be the theme or idea of the dream)*

2. How did you feel? _____ *(Afraid, happy, lost, confused, happy, angry, etc.)*

3. Describe the theme *(What was happening, i.e., on the beach, fighting, running, at a party, Day or night, sunny, raining, etc).*

_____

_____

_____

_____

_____

4. List every symbol *(Sofa, water, pool, shoe, dirt, car, truck, dog, mom, dad, sister, etc.)*

A._____   B._____

C._____   D._____

E._____   F._____

G._____   H._____

5. Describe the dream in detail, including its conclusion *(List every color and number that you remember)*

_____

_____

_____

_____

_____

6. Name and describe the individuals in your dream. *(If you do not know the person, state their role in your dream.)*

Their role in the dream   Who are they to you?

A. _____   _____

B. _____   _____

C. _____   _____

D. _____   _____

7. Describe any project(s) you are currently working on?

_____

_____

_____

_____

_____

8. Briefly describe something you encountered the day before you had this dream.

_____

_____

_____

_____

_____

9. What did you have on your mind before falling asleep on the night you had this dream?

_____

_____

_____

_____

_____

https://shifttothereal.com/idreammagus/

Date: _____ (Enter the date of your dream.)

1. Name the dream: _____ *(This name will typically be the theme or idea of the dream)*

2. How did you feel? _____ *(Afraid, happy, lost, confused, happy, angry, etc.)*

3. Describe the theme *(What was happening, i.e., on the beach, fighting, running, at a party, Day or night, sunny, raining, etc).*

_____

_____

_____

_____

_____

4. List every symbol *(Sofa, water, pool, shoe, dirt, car, truck, dog, mom, dad, sister, etc.)*

A._____   B._____

C._____   D._____

E._____   F._____

G._____   H._____

5. Describe the dream in detail, including its conclusion *(List every color and number that you remember)*

_____

_____

_____

_____

_____

6. Name and describe the individuals in your dream. *(If you do not know the person, state their role in your dream.)*

Their role in the dream	Who are they to you?
A. _____	_____
B. _____	_____
C. _____	_____
D. _____	_____

7. Describe any project(s) you are currently working on?

_____

_____

_____

_____

_____

8. Briefly describe something you encountered the day before you had this dream.

_____

_____

_____

_____

_____

9. What did you have on your mind before falling asleep on the night you had this dream?

_____

_____

_____

_____

_____

https://shifttothereal.com/idreammagus/

Date: _____ (Enter the date of your dream.)

1. Name the dream: _____ *(This name will typically be the theme or idea of the dream)*

2. How did you feel? _____ *(Afraid, happy, lost, confused, happy, angry, etc.)*

3. Describe the theme *(What was happening, i.e., on the beach, fighting, running, at a party, Day or night, sunny, raining, etc).*

_____

_____

_____

_____

_____

4. List every symbol *(Sofa, water, pool, shoe, dirt, car, truck, dog, mom, dad, sister, etc.)*

A._____   B._____

C._____   D._____

E._____   F._____

G._____   H._____

5. Describe the dream in detail, including its conclusion *(List every color and number that you remember)*

_____

_____

_____

_____

_____

6. Name and describe the individuals in your dream. *(If you do not know the person, state their role in your dream.)*

        Their role in the dream   Who are they to you?

A. _____   _____

B. _____   _____

C. _____   _____

D. _____   _____

7. Describe any project(s) you are currently working on?

_____

_____

_____

_____

_____

8. Briefly describe something you encountered the day before you had this dream.

_____

_____

_____

_____

_____

9. What did you have on your mind before falling asleep on the night you had this dream?

_____

_____

_____

_____

_____

Date: _____ (Enter the date of your dream.)

1. Name the dream: _____ *(This name will typically be the theme or idea of the dream)*

2. How did you feel? _____ *(Afraid, happy, lost, confused, happy, angry, etc.)*

3. Describe the theme *(What was happening, i.e., on the beach, fighting, running, at a party, Day or night, sunny, raining, etc).*

_____

_____

_____

_____

_____

4. List every symbol *(Sofa, water, pool, shoe, dirt, car, truck, dog, mom, dad, sister, etc.)*

A._____   B._____

C._____   D._____

E._____   F._____

G._____   H._____

5. Describe the dream in detail, including its conclusion *(List every color and number that you remember)*

_____

_____

_____

_____

_____

6. Name and describe the individuals in your dream. *(If you do not know the person, state their role in your dream.)*

       Their role in the dream   Who are they to you?

A. _____   _____

B. _____   _____

C. _____   _____

D. _____   _____

7. Describe any project(s) you are currently working on?

_____

_____

_____

_____

_____

8. Briefly describe something you encountered the day before you had this dream.

_____

_____

_____

_____

_____

9. What did you have on your mind before falling asleep on the night you had this dream?

_____

_____

_____

_____

_____

                                               https://shifttothereal.com/idreammagus/

Date: _____ (Enter the date of your dream.)

1. Name the dream: _____ (*This name will typically be the theme or idea of the dream*)

2. How did you feel? _____ (*Afraid, happy, lost, confused, happy, angry, etc.*)

3. Describe the theme (*What was happening, i.e., on the beach, fighting, running, at a party, Day or night, sunny, raining, etc*).

_____

_____

_____

_____

_____

4. List every symbol (*Sofa, water, pool, shoe, dirt, car, truck, dog, mom, dad, sister, etc.*)

A._____   B._____

C._____   D._____

E._____   F._____

G._____   H._____

5. Describe the dream in detail, including its conclusion (*List every color and number that you remember*)

_____

_____

_____

_____

_____

6. Name and describe the individuals in your dream. *(If you do not know the person, state their role in your dream.)*

Their role in the dream | Who are they to you?

A. _____   _____

B. _____   _____

C. _____   _____

D. _____   _____

7. Describe any project(s) you are currently working on?

_____

_____

_____

_____

_____

8. Briefly describe something you encountered the day before you had this dream.

_____

_____

_____

_____

_____

9. What did you have on your mind before falling asleep on the night you had this dream?

_____

_____

_____

_____

_____

Date: _____ (Enter the date of your dream.)

1. Name the dream: _____ *(This name will typically be the theme or idea of the dream)*

2. How did you feel? _____ *(Afraid, happy, lost, confused, happy, angry, etc.)*

3. Describe the theme *(What was happening, i.e., on the beach, fighting, running, at a party, Day or night, sunny, raining, etc).*

_____

_____

_____

_____

_____

4. List every symbol *(Sofa, water, pool, shoe, dirt, car, truck, dog, mom, dad, sister, etc.)*

A._____   B._____

C._____   D._____

E._____   F._____

G._____   H._____

5. Describe the dream in detail, including its conclusion *(List every color and number that you remember)*

_____

_____

_____

_____

_____

6. Name and describe the individuals in your dream. *(If you do not know the person, state their role in your dream.)*

Their role in the dream	Who are they to you?
A. _____	_____
B. _____	_____
C. _____	_____
D. _____	_____

7. Describe any project(s) you are currently working on?

_____

_____

_____

_____

_____

8. Briefly describe something you encountered the day before you had this dream.

_____

_____

_____

_____

_____

9. What did you have on your mind before falling asleep on the night you had this dream?

_____

_____

_____

_____

_____

https://shifttothereal.com/idreammagus/

Date: _____ (Enter the date of your dream.)

1. Name the dream: _____ (*This name will typically be the theme or idea of the dream*)

2. How did you feel? _____ (*Afraid, happy, lost, confused, happy, angry, etc.*)

3. Describe the theme (*What was happening, i.e., on the beach, fighting, running, at a party, Day or night, sunny, raining, etc*).

_____

_____

_____

_____

_____

4. List every symbol (*Sofa, water, pool, shoe, dirt, car, truck, dog, mom, dad, sister, etc.*)

A._____   B._____

C._____   D._____

E._____   F._____

G._____   H._____

5. Describe the dream in detail, including its conclusion (*List every color and number that you remember*)

_____

_____

_____

_____

_____

6. Name and describe the individuals in your dream. *(If you do not know the person, state their role in your dream.)*

	Their role in the dream	Who are they to you?
A.	_____	_____
B.	_____	_____
C.	_____	_____
D.	_____	_____

7. Describe any project(s) you are currently working on?

_____

_____

_____

_____

_____

8. Briefly describe something you encountered the day before you had this dream.

_____

_____

_____

_____

_____

9. What did you have on your mind before falling asleep on the night you had this dream?

_____

_____

_____

_____

_____

Date: _____ (Enter the date of your dream.)

1. Name the dream: _____ *(This name will typically be the theme or idea of the dream)*

2. How did you feel? _____ *(Afraid, happy, lost, confused, happy, angry, etc.)*

3. Describe the theme *(What was happening, i.e., on the beach, fighting, running, at a party, Day or night, sunny, raining, etc).*

_____
_____
_____
_____
_____

4. List every symbol *(Sofa, water, pool, shoe, dirt, car, truck, dog, mom, dad, sister, etc.)*

A._____ B._____
C._____ D._____
E._____ F._____
G._____ H._____

5. Describe the dream in detail, including its conclusion *(List every color and number that you remember)*

_____
_____
_____
_____
_____

6. Name and describe the individuals in your dream. *(If you do not know the person, state their role in your dream.)*

Their role in the dream   Who are they to you?

A. _____   _____

B. _____   _____

C. _____   _____

D. _____   _____

7. Describe any project(s) you are currently working on?

_____

_____

_____

_____

_____

8. Briefly describe something you encountered the day before you had this dream.

_____

_____

_____

_____

_____

9. What did you have on your mind before falling asleep on the night you had this dream?

_____

_____

_____

_____

_____

Date: _____ (Enter the date of your dream.)

1. Name the dream: _____ *(This name will typically be the theme or idea of the dream)*

2. How did you feel? _____ *(Afraid, happy, lost, confused, happy, angry, etc.)*

3. Describe the theme *(What was happening, i.e., on the beach, fighting, running, at a party, Day or night, sunny, raining, etc).*

_____
_____
_____
_____
_____

4. List every symbol *(Sofa, water, pool, shoe, dirt, car, truck, dog, mom, dad, sister, etc.)*

A._____   B._____
C._____   D._____
E._____   F._____
G._____   H._____

5. Describe the dream in detail, including its conclusion *(List every color and number that you remember)*

_____
_____
_____
_____
_____

6. Name and describe the individuals in your dream. *(If you do not know the person, state their role in your dream.)*

       Their role in the dream   Who are they to you?

A. _____   _____

B. _____   _____

C. _____   _____

D. _____   _____

7. Describe any project(s) you are currently working on?

_____

_____

_____

_____

_____

8. Briefly describe something you encountered the day before you had this dream.

_____

_____

_____

_____

_____

9. What did you have on your mind before falling asleep on the night you had this dream?

_____

_____

_____

_____

_____

                                             https://shifttothereal.com/idreammagus/

Date: _____ (Enter the date of your dream.)

1. Name the dream: _____ *(This name will typically be the theme or idea of the dream)*

2. How did you feel? _____ *(Afraid, happy, lost, confused, happy, angry, etc.)*

3. Describe the theme *(What was happening, i.e., on the beach, fighting, running, at a party, Day or night, sunny, raining, etc).*

_____

_____

_____

_____

_____

4. List every symbol *(Sofa, water, pool, shoe, dirt, car, truck, dog, mom, dad, sister, etc.)*

A._____   B._____

C._____   D._____

E._____   F._____

G._____   H._____

5. Describe the dream in detail, including its conclusion *(List every color and number that you remember)*

_____

_____

_____

_____

_____

6. Name and describe the individuals in your dream. *(If you do not know the person, state their role in your dream.)*

            Their role in the dream   Who are they to you?

A. _____   _____

B. _____   _____

C. _____   _____

D. _____   _____

7. Describe any project(s) you are currently working on?

_____

_____

_____

_____

_____

8. Briefly describe something you encountered the day before you had this dream.

_____

_____

_____

_____

_____

9. What did you have on your mind before falling asleep on the night you had this dream?

_____

_____

_____

_____

_____

https://shifttothereal.com/idreammagus/

Date: _____ (Enter the date of your dream.)

1. Name the dream: _____ *(This name will typically be the theme or idea of the dream)*

2. How did you feel? _____ *(Afraid, happy, lost, confused, happy, angry, etc.)*

3. Describe the theme *(What was happening, i.e., on the beach, fighting, running, at a party, Day or night, sunny, raining, etc).*

_____

_____

_____

_____

_____

4. List every symbol *(Sofa, water, pool, shoe, dirt, car, truck, dog, mom, dad, sister, etc.)*

   A._____   B._____

   C._____   D._____

   E._____   F._____

   G._____   H._____

5. Describe the dream in detail, including its conclusion *(List every color and number that you remember)*

_____

_____

_____

_____

_____

6. Name and describe the individuals in your dream. *(If you do not know the person, state their role in your dream.)*

Their role in the dream	Who are they to you?
A. _____	_____
B. _____	_____
C. _____	_____
D. _____	_____

7. Describe any project(s) you are currently working on?

_____

_____

_____

_____

_____

8. Briefly describe something you encountered the day before you had this dream.

_____

_____

_____

_____

_____

9. What did you have on your mind before falling asleep on the night you had this dream?

_____

_____

_____

_____

_____

https://shifttothereal.com/idreammagus/

Date: _____ (Enter the date of your dream.)

1. Name the dream: _____ *(This name will typically be the theme or idea of the dream)*

2. How did you feel? _____ *(Afraid, happy, lost, confused, happy, angry, etc.)*

3. Describe the theme *(What was happening, i.e., on the beach, fighting, running, at a party, Day or night, sunny, raining, etc).*

_____

_____

_____

_____

_____

4. List every symbol *(Sofa, water, pool, shoe, dirt, car, truck, dog, mom, dad, sister, etc.)*

A._____   B._____

C._____   D._____

E._____   F._____

G._____   H._____

5. Describe the dream in detail, including its conclusion *(List every color and number that you remember)*

_____

_____

_____

_____

_____

6. Name and describe the individuals in your dream. *(If you do not know the person, state their role in your dream.)*

Their role in the dream	Who are they to you?
A. _____	_____
B. _____	_____
C. _____	_____
D. _____	_____

7. Describe any project(s) you are currently working on?

_____

_____

_____

_____

_____

8. Briefly describe something you encountered the day before you had this dream.

_____

_____

_____

_____

_____

9. What did you have on your mind before falling asleep on the night you had this dream?

_____

_____

_____

_____

_____

Date: _____ (Enter the date of your dream.)

1. Name the dream: _____ *(This name will typically be the theme or idea of the dream)*

2. How did you feel? _____ *(Afraid, happy, lost, confused, happy, angry, etc.)*

3. Describe the theme *(What was happening, i.e., on the beach, fighting, running, at a party, Day or night, sunny, raining, etc).*

_____
_____
_____
_____
_____

4. List every symbol *(Sofa, water, pool, shoe, dirt, car, truck, dog, mom, dad, sister, etc.)*

A._____ B._____
C._____ D._____
E._____ F._____
G._____ H._____

5. Describe the dream in detail, including its conclusion *(List every color and number that you remember)*

_____
_____
_____
_____
_____

6. Name and describe the individuals in your dream. *(If you do not know the person, state their role in your dream.)*

	Their role in the dream	Who are they to you?
A.	_____	_____
B.	_____	_____
C.	_____	_____
D.	_____	_____

7. Describe any project(s) you are currently working on?

_____

_____

_____

_____

_____

8. Briefly describe something you encountered the day before you had this dream.

_____

_____

_____

_____

_____

9. What did you have on your mind before falling asleep on the night you had this dream?

_____

_____

_____

_____

_____

https://shifttothereal.com/idreammagus/

Date: _____ (Enter the date of your dream.)

1. Name the dream: _____ *(This name will typically be the theme or idea of the dream)*

2. How did you feel? _____ *(Afraid, happy, lost, confused, happy, angry, etc.)*

3. Describe the theme *(What was happening, i.e., on the beach, fighting, running, at a party, Day or night, sunny, raining, etc).*

_____

_____

_____

_____

_____

_____

4. List every symbol *(Sofa, water, pool, shoe, dirt, car, truck, dog, mom, dad, sister, etc.)*

A._____   B._____

C._____   D._____

E._____   F._____

G._____   H._____

5. Describe the dream in detail, including its conclusion *(List every color and number that you remember)*

_____

_____

_____

_____

_____

_____

6. Name and describe the individuals in your dream. *(If you do not know the person, state their role in your dream.)*

        Their role in the dream   Who are they to you?

A. _____   _____

B. _____   _____

C. _____   _____

D. _____   _____

7. Describe any project(s) you are currently working on?

_____

_____

_____

_____

_____

8. Briefly describe something you encountered the day before you had this dream.

_____

_____

_____

_____

_____

9. What did you have on your mind before falling asleep on the night you had this dream?

_____

_____

_____

_____

_____

https://shifttothereal.com/idreammagus/

Date: _____ (Enter the date of your dream.)

1. Name the dream: _____ (*This name will typically be the theme or idea of the dream*)

2. How did you feel? _____ (*Afraid, happy, lost, confused, happy, angry, etc.*)

3. Describe the theme (*What was happening, i.e., on the beach, fighting, running, at a party, Day or night, sunny, raining, etc*).

_____

_____

_____

_____

_____

4. List every symbol (*Sofa, water, pool, shoe, dirt, car, truck, dog, mom, dad, sister, etc.*)

A._____   B._____

C._____   D._____

E._____   F._____

G._____   H._____

5. Describe the dream in detail, including its conclusion (*List every color and number that you remember*)

_____

_____

_____

_____

_____

6. Name and describe the individuals in your dream. *(If you do not know the person, state their role in your dream.)*

        Their role in the dream   Who are they to you?

A. _____   _____

B. _____   _____

C. _____   _____

D. _____   _____

7. Describe any project(s) you are currently working on?

_____

_____

_____

_____

_____

8. Briefly describe something you encountered the day before you had this dream.

_____

_____

_____

_____

_____

9. What did you have on your mind before falling asleep on the night you had this dream?

_____

_____

_____

_____

_____

Date: _____ (Enter the date of your dream.)

1. Name the dream: _____ *(This name will typically be the theme or idea of the dream)*

2. How did you feel? _____ *(Afraid, happy, lost, confused, happy, angry, etc.)*

3. Describe the theme *(What was happening, i.e., on the beach, fighting, running, at a party, Day or night, sunny, raining, etc).*

_____

_____

_____

_____

_____

4. List every symbol *(Sofa, water, pool, shoe, dirt, car, truck, dog, mom, dad, sister, etc.)*

A._____   B._____

C._____   D._____

E._____   F._____

G._____   H._____

5. Describe the dream in detail, including its conclusion *(List every color and number that you remember)*

_____

_____

_____

_____

_____

6. Name and describe the individuals in your dream. *(If you do not know the person, state their role in your dream.)*

        Their role in the dream   Who are they to you?

A. _____   _____

B. _____   _____

C. _____   _____

D. _____   _____

7. Describe any project(s) you are currently working on?

_____

_____

_____

_____

_____

8. Briefly describe something you encountered the day before you had this dream.

_____

_____

_____

_____

_____

9. What did you have on your mind before falling asleep on the night you had this dream?

_____

_____

_____

_____

_____

https://shifttothereal.com/idreammagus/

✳ A DREAM CATCHER'S JOURNAL ✳

Date: _____ (Enter the date of your dream.)

1. Name the dream: _____ *(This name will typically be the theme or idea of the dream)*

2. How did you feel? _____ *(Afraid, happy, lost, confused, happy, angry, etc.)*

3. Describe the theme *(What was happening, i.e., on the beach, fighting, running, at a party, Day or night, sunny, raining, etc).*

_____

_____

_____

_____

_____

4. List every symbol *(Sofa, water, pool, shoe, dirt, car, truck, dog, mom, dad, sister, etc.)*

A._____   B._____

C._____   D._____

E._____   F._____

G._____   H._____

5. Describe the dream in detail, including its conclusion *(List every color and number that you remember)*

_____

_____

_____

_____

_____

6. Name and describe the individuals in your dream. *(If you do not know the person, state their role in your dream.)*

Their role in the dream   Who are they to you?

A. _____   _____

B. _____   _____

C. _____   _____

D. _____   _____

7. Describe any project(s) you are currently working on?

_____

_____

_____

_____

_____

8. Briefly describe something you encountered the day before you had this dream.

_____

_____

_____

_____

_____

9. What did you have on your mind before falling asleep on the night you had this dream?

_____

_____

_____

_____

_____

Date: _____ (Enter the date of your dream.)

1. Name the dream: _____ *(This name will typically be the theme or idea of the dream)*

2. How did you feel? _____ *(Afraid, happy, lost, confused, happy, angry, etc.)*

3. Describe the theme *(What was happening, i.e., on the beach, fighting, running, at a party, Day or night, sunny, raining, etc).*

_____

_____

_____

_____

_____

4. List every symbol *(Sofa, water, pool, shoe, dirt, car, truck, dog, mom, dad, sister, etc.)*

A._____   B._____

C._____   D._____

E._____   F._____

G._____   H._____

5. Describe the dream in detail, including its conclusion *(List every color and number that you remember)*

_____

_____

_____

_____

_____

6. Name and describe the individuals in your dream. *(If you do not know the person, state their role in your dream.)*

Their role in the dream   Who are they to you?

A. _____   _____

B. _____   _____

C. _____   _____

D. _____   _____

7. Describe any project(s) you are currently working on?

_____

_____

_____

_____

_____

8. Briefly describe something you encountered the day before you had this dream.

_____

_____

_____

_____

_____

9. What did you have on your mind before falling asleep on the night you had this dream?

_____

_____

_____

_____

_____

Date: _____ (Enter the date of your dream.)

1. Name the dream: _____ *(This name will typically be the theme or idea of the dream)*

2. How did you feel? _____ *(Afraid, happy, lost, confused, happy, angry, etc.)*

3. Describe the theme *(What was happening, i.e., on the beach, fighting, running, at a party, Day or night, sunny, raining, etc).*

_____

_____

_____

_____

_____

4. List every symbol *(Sofa, water, pool, shoe, dirt, car, truck, dog, mom, dad, sister, etc.)*

A._____   B._____

C._____   D._____

E._____   F._____

G._____   H._____

5. Describe the dream in detail, including its conclusion *(List every color and number that you remember)*

_____

_____

_____

_____

_____

6. Name and describe the individuals in your dream. *(If you do not know the person, state their role in your dream.)*

Their role in the dream   Who are they to you?

A. _____   _____

B. _____   _____

C. _____   _____

D. _____   _____

7. Describe any project(s) you are currently working on?

_____

_____

_____

_____

_____

8. Briefly describe something you encountered the day before you had this dream.

_____

_____

_____

_____

_____

9. What did you have on your mind before falling asleep on the night you had this dream?

_____

_____

_____

_____

_____

https://shifttothereal.com/idreammagus/

Date: _____ (Enter the date of your dream.)

1. Name the dream: _____ *(This name will typically be the theme or idea of the dream)*

2. How did you feel? _____ *(Afraid, happy, lost, confused, happy, angry, etc.)*

3. Describe the theme *(What was happening, i.e., on the beach, fighting, running, at a party, Day or night, sunny, raining, etc).*

_____

_____

_____

_____

_____

4. List every symbol *(Sofa, water, pool, shoe, dirt, car, truck, dog, mom, dad, sister, etc.)*

A._____   B._____

C._____   D._____

E._____   F._____

G._____   H._____

5. Describe the dream in detail, including its conclusion *(List every color and number that you remember)*

_____

_____

_____

_____

_____

6. Name and describe the individuals in your dream. *(If you do not know the person, state their role in your dream.)*

      Their role in the dream   Who are they to you?

A. _____   _____

B. _____   _____

C. _____   _____

D. _____   _____

7. Describe any project(s) you are currently working on?

_____

_____

_____

_____

_____

8. Briefly describe something you encountered the day before you had this dream.

_____

_____

_____

_____

_____

9. What did you have on your mind before falling asleep on the night you had this dream?

_____

_____

_____

_____

_____

Date: _____ (Enter the date of your dream.)

1. Name the dream: _____ *(This name will typically be the theme or idea of the dream)*

2. How did you feel? _____ *(Afraid, happy, lost, confused, happy, angry, etc.)*

3. Describe the theme *(What was happening, i.e., on the beach, fighting, running, at a party, Day or night, sunny, raining, etc).*

_____

_____

_____

_____

_____

4. List every symbol *(Sofa, water, pool, shoe, dirt, car, truck, dog, mom, dad, sister, etc.)*

A._____   B._____

C._____   D._____

E._____   F._____

G._____   H._____

5. Describe the dream in detail, including its conclusion *(List every color and number that you remember)*

_____

_____

_____

_____

_____

6. Name and describe the individuals in your dream. *(If you do not know the person, state their role in your dream.)*

        Their role in the dream   Who are they to you?

A. _____   _____

B. _____   _____

C. _____   _____

D. _____   _____

7. Describe any project(s) you are currently working on?

_____

_____

_____

_____

_____

8. Briefly describe something you encountered the day before you had this dream.

_____

_____

_____

_____

_____

9. What did you have on your mind before falling asleep on the night you had this dream?

_____

_____

_____

_____

_____

Date: _____ (Enter the date of your dream.)

1. Name the dream: _____ *(This name will typically be the theme or idea of the dream)*

2. How did you feel? _____ *(Afraid, happy, lost, confused, happy, angry, etc.)*

3. Describe the theme *(What was happening, i.e., on the beach, fighting, running, at a party, Day or night, sunny, raining, etc).*

_____

_____

_____

_____

_____

4. List every symbol *(Sofa, water, pool, shoe, dirt, car, truck, dog, mom, dad, sister, etc.)*

A._____   B._____

C._____   D._____

E._____   F._____

G._____   H._____

5. Describe the dream in detail, including its conclusion *(List every color and number that you remember)*

_____

_____

_____

_____

_____

6. Name and describe the individuals in your dream. *(If you do not know the person, state their role in your dream.)*

           Their role in the dream   Who are they to you?

    A. _____   _____

    B. _____   _____

    C. _____   _____

    D. _____   _____

7. Describe any project(s) you are currently working on?

_____

_____

_____

_____

_____

8. Briefly describe something you encountered the day before you had this dream.

_____

_____

_____

_____

_____

9. What did you have on your mind before falling asleep on the night you had this dream?

_____

_____

_____

_____

_____

                                                   https://shifttothereal.com/idreammagus/

Date: _____ (Enter the date of your dream.)

1. Name the dream: _____ *(This name will typically be the theme or idea of the dream)*

2. How did you feel? _____ *(Afraid, happy, lost, confused, happy, angry, etc.)*

3. Describe the theme *(What was happening, i.e., on the beach, fighting, running, at a party, Day or night, sunny, raining, etc).*

_____

_____

_____

_____

_____

4. List every symbol *(Sofa, water, pool, shoe, dirt, car, truck, dog, mom, dad, sister, etc.)*

   A._____   B._____

   C._____   D._____

   E._____   F._____

   G._____   H._____

5. Describe the dream in detail, including its conclusion *(List every color and number that you remember)*

_____

_____

_____

_____

_____

6. Name and describe the individuals in your dream. *(If you do not know the person, state their role in your dream.)*

        Their role in the dream   Who are they to you?

    A. _____   _____

    B. _____   _____

    C. _____   _____

    D. _____   _____

7. Describe any project(s) you are currently working on?

_____

_____

_____

_____

_____

8. Briefly describe something you encountered the day before you had this dream.

_____

_____

_____

_____

_____

9. What did you have on your mind before falling asleep on the night you had this dream?

_____

_____

_____

_____

_____

                https://shifttothereal.com/idreammagus/

Date: _____ (Enter the date of your dream.)

1. Name the dream: _____ *(This name will typically be the theme or idea of the dream)*

2. How did you feel? _____ *(Afraid, happy, lost, confused, happy, angry, etc.)*

3. Describe the theme *(What was happening, i.e., on the beach, fighting, running, at a party, Day or night, sunny, raining, etc).*

_____

_____

_____

_____

_____

4. List every symbol *(Sofa, water, pool, shoe, dirt, car, truck, dog, mom, dad, sister, etc.)*

A._____   B._____

C._____   D._____

E._____   F._____

G._____   H._____

5. Describe the dream in detail, including its conclusion *(List every color and number that you remember)*

_____

_____

_____

_____

_____

6. Name and describe the individuals in your dream. *(If you do not know the person, state their role in your dream.)*

      Their role in the dream   Who are they to you?

    A. _____   _____

    B. _____   _____

    C. _____   _____

    D. _____   _____

7. Describe any project(s) you are currently working on?

_____

_____

_____

_____

_____

8. Briefly describe something you encountered the day before you had this dream.

_____

_____

_____

_____

_____

9. What did you have on your mind before falling asleep on the night you had this dream?

_____

_____

_____

_____

_____

Date: _____ (Enter the date of your dream.)

1. Name the dream: _____ *(This name will typically be the theme or idea of the dream)*

2. How did you feel? _____ *(Afraid, happy, lost, confused, happy, angry, etc.)*

3. Describe the theme *(What was happening, i.e., on the beach, fighting, running, at a party, Day or night, sunny, raining, etc).*

_____

_____

_____

_____

_____

4. List every symbol *(Sofa, water, pool, shoe, dirt, car, truck, dog, mom, dad, sister, etc.)*

   A._____   B._____

   C._____   D._____

   E._____   F._____

   G._____   H._____

5. Describe the dream in detail, including its conclusion *(List every color and number that you remember)*

_____

_____

_____

_____

_____

6. Name and describe the individuals in your dream. *(If you do not know the person, state their role in your dream.)*

Their role in the dream   Who are they to you?

A. _____   _____

B. _____   _____

C. _____   _____

D. _____   _____

7. Describe any project(s) you are currently working on?

_____

_____

_____

_____

_____

8. Briefly describe something you encountered the day before you had this dream.

_____

_____

_____

_____

_____

9. What did you have on your mind before falling asleep on the night you had this dream?

_____

_____

_____

_____

_____

Date: _____ (Enter the date of your dream.)

1. Name the dream: _____ *(This name will typically be the theme or idea of the dream)*

2. How did you feel? _____ *(Afraid, happy, lost, confused, happy, angry, etc.)*

3. Describe the theme *(What was happening, i.e., on the beach, fighting, running, at a party, Day or night, sunny, raining, etc).*

_____

_____

_____

_____

_____

4. List every symbol *(Sofa, water, pool, shoe, dirt, car, truck, dog, mom, dad, sister, etc.)*

A._____   B._____

C._____   D._____

E._____   F._____

G._____   H._____

5. Describe the dream in detail, including its conclusion *(List every color and number that you remember)*

_____

_____

_____

_____

_____

6. Name and describe the individuals in your dream. *(If you do not know the person, state their role in your dream.)*

Their role in the dream	Who are they to you?
A. _____	_____
B. _____	_____
C. _____	_____
D. _____	_____

7. Describe any project(s) you are currently working on?

_____

_____

_____

_____

_____

8. Briefly describe something you encountered the day before you had this dream.

_____

_____

_____

_____

_____

9. What did you have on your mind before falling asleep on the night you had this dream?

_____

_____

_____

_____

_____

https://shifttothereal.com/idreammagus/

Date: _____ (Enter the date of your dream.)

1. Name the dream: _____ *(This name will typically be the theme or idea of the dream)*

2. How did you feel? _____ *(Afraid, happy, lost, confused, happy, angry, etc.)*

3. Describe the theme *(What was happening, i.e., on the beach, fighting, running, at a party, Day or night, sunny, raining, etc).*

_____

_____

_____

_____

_____

4. List every symbol *(Sofa, water, pool, shoe, dirt, car, truck, dog, mom, dad, sister, etc.)*

A._____   B._____

C._____   D._____

E._____   F._____

G._____   H._____

5. Describe the dream in detail, including its conclusion *(List every color and number that you remember)*

_____

_____

_____

_____

_____

6. Name and describe the individuals in your dream. *(If you do not know the person, state their role in your dream.)*

        Their role in the dream   Who are they to you?

A. _____   _____

B. _____   _____

C. _____   _____

D. _____   _____

7. Describe any project(s) you are currently working on?

_____

_____

_____

_____

_____

8. Briefly describe something you encountered the day before you had this dream.

_____

_____

_____

_____

_____

9. What did you have on your mind before falling asleep on the night you had this dream?

_____

_____

_____

_____

_____

Date: _____ (Enter the date of your dream.)

1. Name the dream: _____ *(This name will typically be the theme or idea of the dream)*

2. How did you feel? _____ *(Afraid, happy, lost, confused, happy, angry, etc.)*

3. Describe the theme *(What was happening, i.e., on the beach, fighting, running, at a party, Day or night, sunny, raining, etc).*

_____

_____

_____

_____

_____

4. List every symbol *(Sofa, water, pool, shoe, dirt, car, truck, dog, mom, dad, sister, etc.)*

A._____   B._____

C._____   D._____

E._____   F._____

G._____   H._____

5. Describe the dream in detail, including its conclusion *(List every color and number that you remember)*

_____

_____

_____

_____

_____

6. Name and describe the individuals in your dream. *(If you do not know the person, state their role in your dream.)*

           Their role in the dream   Who are they to you?

A. _____   _____

B. _____   _____

C. _____   _____

D. _____   _____

7. Describe any project(s) you are currently working on?

_____

_____

_____

_____

_____

8. Briefly describe something you encountered the day before you had this dream.

_____

_____

_____

_____

_____

9. What did you have on your mind before falling asleep on the night you had this dream?

_____

_____

_____

_____

_____

Date: _____ (Enter the date of your dream.)

1. Name the dream: _____ *(This name will typically be the theme or idea of the dream)*

2. How did you feel? _____ *(Afraid, happy, lost, confused, happy, angry, etc.)*

3. Describe the theme *(What was happening, i.e., on the beach, fighting, running, at a party, Day or night, sunny, raining, etc).*

_____

_____

_____

_____

_____

4. List every symbol *(Sofa, water, pool, shoe, dirt, car, truck, dog, mom, dad, sister, etc.)*

A._____   B._____

C._____   D._____

E._____   F._____

G._____   H._____

5. Describe the dream in detail, including its conclusion *(List every color and number that you remember)*

_____

_____

_____

_____

_____

6. Name and describe the individuals in your dream. *(If you do not know the person, state their role in your dream.)*

Their role in the dream   Who are they to you?

A. _____   _____

B. _____   _____

C. _____   _____

D. _____   _____

7. Describe any project(s) you are currently working on?

_____

_____

_____

_____

_____

8. Briefly describe something you encountered the day before you had this dream.

_____

_____

_____

_____

_____

9. What did you have on your mind before falling asleep on the night you had this dream?

_____

_____

_____

_____

_____

https://shifttothereal.com/idreammagus/

Date: _____ (Enter the date of your dream.)

1. Name the dream: _____ *(This name will typically be the theme or idea of the dream)*

2. How did you feel? _____ *(Afraid, happy, lost, confused, happy, angry, etc.)*

3. Describe the theme *(What was happening, i.e., on the beach, fighting, running, at a party, Day or night, sunny, raining, etc).*

_____
_____
_____
_____
_____

4. List every symbol *(Sofa, water, pool, shoe, dirt, car, truck, dog, mom, dad, sister, etc.)*

A._____ B._____
C._____ D._____
E._____ F._____
G._____ H._____

5. Describe the dream in detail, including its conclusion *(List every color and number that you remember)*

_____
_____
_____
_____
_____

6. Name and describe the individuals in your dream. *(If you do not know the person, state their role in your dream.)*

        Their role in the dream   Who are they to you?

A. _____   _____

B. _____   _____

C. _____   _____

D. _____   _____

7. Describe any project(s) you are currently working on?

_____

_____

_____

_____

_____

8. Briefly describe something you encountered the day before you had this dream.

_____

_____

_____

_____

_____

9. What did you have on your mind before falling asleep on the night you had this dream?

_____

_____

_____

_____

_____

Date: _____ (Enter the date of your dream.)

1. Name the dream: _____ *(This name will typically be the theme or idea of the dream)*

2. How did you feel? _____ *(Afraid, happy, lost, confused, happy, angry, etc.)*

3. Describe the theme *(What was happening, i.e., on the beach, fighting, running, at a party, Day or night, sunny, raining, etc).*

_____

_____

_____

_____

_____

4. List every symbol *(Sofa, water, pool, shoe, dirt, car, truck, dog, mom, dad, sister, etc.)*

A._____   B._____

C._____   D._____

E._____   F._____

G._____   H._____

5. Describe the dream in detail, including its conclusion *(List every color and number that you remember)*

_____

_____

_____

_____

_____

6. Name and describe the individuals in your dream. *(If you do not know the person, state their role in your dream.)*

Their role in the dream | Who are they to you?

A. _____ _____

B. _____ _____

C. _____ _____

D. _____ _____

7. Describe any project(s) you are currently working on?

_____

_____

_____

_____

_____

8. Briefly describe something you encountered the day before you had this dream.

_____

_____

_____

_____

_____

9. What did you have on your mind before falling asleep on the night you had this dream?

_____

_____

_____

_____

_____

https://shifttothereal.com/idreammagus/

Date: _____ (Enter the date of your dream.)

1. Name the dream: _____ *(This name will typically be the theme or idea of the dream)*

2. How did you feel? _____ *(Afraid, happy, lost, confused, happy, angry, etc.)*

3. Describe the theme *(What was happening, i.e., on the beach, fighting, running, at a party, Day or night, sunny, raining, etc).*

_____

_____

_____

_____

_____

4. List every symbol *(Sofa, water, pool, shoe, dirt, car, truck, dog, mom, dad, sister, etc.)*

A._____   B._____

C._____   D._____

E._____   F._____

G._____   H._____

5. Describe the dream in detail, including its conclusion *(List every color and number that you remember)*

_____

_____

_____

_____

_____

6. Name and describe the individuals in your dream. *(If you do not know the person, state their role in your dream.)*

          Their role in the dream   Who are they to you?

    A. _____   _____

    B. _____   _____

    C. _____   _____

    D. _____   _____

7. Describe any project(s) you are currently working on?

_____

_____

_____

_____

_____

8. Briefly describe something you encountered the day before you had this dream.

_____

_____

_____

_____

_____

9. What did you have on your mind before falling asleep on the night you had this dream?

_____

_____

_____

_____

_____

Date: _____ (Enter the date of your dream.)

1. Name the dream: _____ *(This name will typically be the theme or idea of the dream)*

2. How did you feel? _____ *(Afraid, happy, lost, confused, happy, angry, etc.)*

3. Describe the theme *(What was happening, i.e., on the beach, fighting, running, at a party, Day or night, sunny, raining, etc).*

_____

_____

_____

_____

_____

4. List every symbol *(Sofa, water, pool, shoe, dirt, car, truck, dog, mom, dad, sister, etc.)*

A._____   B._____

C._____   D._____

E._____   F._____

G._____   H._____

5. Describe the dream in detail, including its conclusion *(List every color and number that you remember)*

_____

_____

_____

_____

_____

6. Name and describe the individuals in your dream. *(If you do not know the person, state their role in your dream.)*

        Their role in the dream   Who are they to you?

A. _____   _____

B. _____   _____

C. _____   _____

D. _____   _____

7. Describe any project(s) you are currently working on?

_____

_____

_____

_____

_____

8. Briefly describe something you encountered the day before you had this dream.

_____

_____

_____

_____

_____

9. What did you have on your mind before falling asleep on the night you had this dream?

_____

_____

_____

_____

_____

                                   https://shifttothereal.com/idreammagus/

Date: _____ (Enter the date of your dream.)

1. Name the dream: _____ *(This name will typically be the theme or idea of the dream)*

2. How did you feel? _____ *(Afraid, happy, lost, confused, happy, angry, etc.)*

3. Describe the theme *(What was happening, i.e., on the beach, fighting, running, at a party, Day or night, sunny, raining, etc).*

_____

_____

_____

_____

_____

4. List every symbol *(Sofa, water, pool, shoe, dirt, car, truck, dog, mom, dad, sister, etc.)*

A._____   B._____

C._____   D._____

E._____   F._____

G._____   H._____

5. Describe the dream in detail, including its conclusion *(List every color and number that you remember)*

_____

_____

_____

_____

_____

6. Name and describe the individuals in your dream. *(If you do not know the person, state their role in your dream.)*

       Their role in the dream   Who are they to you?

A. _____   _____

B. _____   _____

C. _____   _____

D. _____   _____

7. Describe any project(s) you are currently working on?

_____

_____

_____

_____

_____

8. Briefly describe something you encountered the day before you had this dream.

_____

_____

_____

_____

_____

9. What did you have on your mind before falling asleep on the night you had this dream?

_____

_____

_____

_____

_____

Date: _____ (Enter the date of your dream.)

1. Name the dream: _____ *(This name will typically be the theme or idea of the dream)*

2. How did you feel? _____ *(Afraid, happy, lost, confused, happy, angry, etc.)*

3. Describe the theme *(What was happening, i.e., on the beach, fighting, running, at a party, Day or night, sunny, raining, etc).*

_____

_____

_____

_____

_____

4. List every symbol *(Sofa, water, pool, shoe, dirt, car, truck, dog, mom, dad, sister, etc.)*

A._____   B._____

C._____   D._____

E._____   F._____

G._____   H._____

5. Describe the dream in detail, including its conclusion *(List every color and number that you remember)*

_____

_____

_____

_____

_____

6. Name and describe the individuals in your dream. *(If you do not know the person, state their role in your dream.)*

Their role in the dream　　　　　Who are they to you?

A. _____　　_____

B. _____　　_____

C. _____　　_____

D. _____　　_____

7. Describe any project(s) you are currently working on?

_____

_____

_____

_____

_____

8. Briefly describe something you encountered the day before you had this dream.

_____

_____

_____

_____

_____

9. What did you have on your mind before falling asleep on the night you had this dream?

_____

_____

_____

_____

_____

Date: _____ (Enter the date of your dream.)

1. Name the dream: _____ *(This name will typically be the theme or idea of the dream)*

2. How did you feel? _____ *(Afraid, happy, lost, confused, happy, angry, etc.)*

3. Describe the theme *(What was happening, i.e., on the beach, fighting, running, at a party, Day or night, sunny, raining, etc).*

_____

_____

_____

_____

_____

4. List every symbol *(Sofa, water, pool, shoe, dirt, car, truck, dog, mom, dad, sister, etc.)*

A._____   B._____

C._____   D._____

E._____   F._____

G._____   H._____

5. Describe the dream in detail, including its conclusion *(List every color and number that you remember)*

_____

_____

_____

_____

_____

6. Name and describe the individuals in your dream. *(If you do not know the person, state their role in your dream.)*

Their role in the dream	Who are they to you?
A. _____	_____
B. _____	_____
C. _____	_____
D. _____	_____

7. Describe any project(s) you are currently working on?

_____

_____

_____

_____

_____

8. Briefly describe something you encountered the day before you had this dream.

_____

_____

_____

_____

_____

9. What did you have on your mind before falling asleep on the night you had this dream?

_____

_____

_____

_____

_____

https://shifttothereal.com/idreammagus/

Date: _____ (Enter the date of your dream.)

1. Name the dream: _____ *(This name will typically be the theme or idea of the dream)*

2. How did you feel? _____ *(Afraid, happy, lost, confused, happy, angry, etc.)*

3. Describe the theme *(What was happening, i.e., on the beach, fighting, running, at a party, Day or night, sunny, raining, etc).*

_____

_____

_____

_____

_____

4. List every symbol *(Sofa, water, pool, shoe, dirt, car, truck, dog, mom, dad, sister, etc.)*

A._____   B._____

C._____   D._____

E._____   F._____

G._____   H._____

5. Describe the dream in detail, including its conclusion *(List every color and number that you remember)*

_____

_____

_____

_____

_____

6. Name and describe the individuals in your dream. *(If you do not know the person, state their role in your dream.)*

Their role in the dream	Who are they to you?
A. _____	_____
B. _____	_____
C. _____	_____
D. _____	_____

7. Describe any project(s) you are currently working on?

_____

_____

_____

_____

_____

8. Briefly describe something you encountered the day before you had this dream.

_____

_____

_____

_____

_____

9. What did you have on your mind before falling asleep on the night you had this dream?

_____

_____

_____

_____

_____

Date: _____ (Enter the date of your dream.)

1. Name the dream: _____ *(This name will typically be the theme or idea of the dream)*

2. How did you feel? _____ *(Afraid, happy, lost, confused, happy, angry, etc.)*

3. Describe the theme *(What was happening, i.e., on the beach, fighting, running, at a party, Day or night, sunny, raining, etc).*

_____

_____

_____

_____

_____

4. List every symbol *(Sofa, water, pool, shoe, dirt, car, truck, dog, mom, dad, sister, etc.)*

A._____   B._____

C._____   D._____

E._____   F._____

G._____   H._____

5. Describe the dream in detail, including its conclusion *(List every color and number that you remember)*

_____

_____

_____

_____

_____

6. Name and describe the individuals in your dream. *(If you do not know the person, state their role in your dream.)*

Their role in the dream   Who are they to you?

A. _____   _____

B. _____   _____

C. _____   _____

D. _____   _____

7. Describe any project(s) you are currently working on?

_____

_____

_____

_____

_____

8. Briefly describe something you encountered the day before you had this dream.

_____

_____

_____

_____

_____

9. What did you have on your mind before falling asleep on the night you had this dream?

_____

_____

_____

_____

_____

Date: _____ (Enter the date of your dream.)

1. Name the dream: _____ *(This name will typically be the theme or idea of the dream)*

2. How did you feel? _____ *(Afraid, happy, lost, confused, happy, angry, etc.)*

3. Describe the theme *(What was happening, i.e., on the beach, fighting, running, at a party, Day or night, sunny, raining, etc).*

_____

_____

_____

_____

_____

4. List every symbol *(Sofa, water, pool, shoe, dirt, car, truck, dog, mom, dad, sister, etc.)*

   A._____   B._____

   C._____   D._____

   E._____   F._____

   G._____   H._____

5. Describe the dream in detail, including its conclusion *(List every color and number that you remember)*

_____

_____

_____

_____

_____

6. Name and describe the individuals in your dream. *(If you do not know the person, state their role in your dream.)*

         Their role in the dream   Who are they to you?

A. _____   _____

B. _____   _____

C. _____   _____

D. _____   _____

7. Describe any project(s) you are currently working on?

_____

_____

_____

_____

_____

8. Briefly describe something you encountered the day before you had this dream.

_____

_____

_____

_____

_____

9. What did you have on your mind before falling asleep on the night you had this dream?

_____

_____

_____

_____

_____

Date: _____ (Enter the date of your dream.)

1. Name the dream: _____ *(This name will typically be the theme or idea of the dream)*

2. How did you feel? _____ *(Afraid, happy, lost, confused, happy, angry, etc.)*

3. Describe the theme *(What was happening, i.e., on the beach, fighting, running, at a party, Day or night, sunny, raining, etc).*

_____

_____

_____

_____

_____

4. List every symbol *(Sofa, water, pool, shoe, dirt, car, truck, dog, mom, dad, sister, etc.)*

A._____   B._____

C._____   D._____

E._____   F._____

G._____   H._____

5. Describe the dream in detail, including its conclusion *(List every color and number that you remember)*

_____

_____

_____

_____

_____

6. Name and describe the individuals in your dream. *(If you do not know the person, state their role in your dream.)*

        Their role in the dream   Who are they to you?

A. _____   _____

B. _____   _____

C. _____   _____

D. _____   _____

7. Describe any project(s) you are currently working on?

_____

_____

_____

_____

_____

8. Briefly describe something you encountered the day before you had this dream.

_____

_____

_____

_____

_____

9. What did you have on your mind before falling asleep on the night you had this dream?

_____

_____

_____

_____

_____

     https://shifttothereal.com/idreammagus/

Date: _____ (Enter the date of your dream.)

1. Name the dream: _____ *(This name will typically be the theme or idea of the dream)*

2. How did you feel? _____ *(Afraid, happy, lost, confused, happy, angry, etc.)*

3. Describe the theme *(What was happening, i.e., on the beach, fighting, running, at a party, Day or night, sunny, raining, etc).*

_____

_____

_____

_____

_____

4. List every symbol *(Sofa, water, pool, shoe, dirt, car, truck, dog, mom, dad, sister, etc.)*

A._____   B._____

C._____   D._____

E._____   F._____

G._____   H._____

5. Describe the dream in detail, including its conclusion *(List every color and number that you remember)*

_____

_____

_____

_____

_____

6. Name and describe the individuals in your dream. *(If you do not know the person, state their role in your dream.)*

	Their role in the dream	Who are they to you?
A.	_____	_____
B.	_____	_____
C.	_____	_____
D.	_____	_____

7. Describe any project(s) you are currently working on?

_____

_____

_____

_____

_____

8. Briefly describe something you encountered the day before you had this dream.

_____

_____

_____

_____

_____

9. What did you have on your mind before falling asleep on the night you had this dream?

_____

_____

_____

_____

_____

https://shifttothereal.com/idreammagus/

Date: _____ (Enter the date of your dream.)

1. Name the dream: _____ *(This name will typically be the theme or idea of the dream)*

2. How did you feel? _____ *(Afraid, happy, lost, confused, happy, angry, etc.)*

3. Describe the theme *(What was happening, i.e., on the beach, fighting, running, at a party, Day or night, sunny, raining, etc).*

_____

_____

_____

_____

_____

4. List every symbol *(Sofa, water, pool, shoe, dirt, car, truck, dog, mom, dad, sister, etc.)*

A._____   B._____

C._____   D._____

E._____   F._____

G._____   H._____

5. Describe the dream in detail, including its conclusion *(List every color and number that you remember)*

_____

_____

_____

_____

_____

6. Name and describe the individuals in your dream. *(If you do not know the person, state their role in your dream.)*

         Their role in the dream   Who are they to you?

A. _____   _____

B. _____   _____

C. _____   _____

D. _____   _____

7. Describe any project(s) you are currently working on?

_____

_____

_____

_____

_____

8. Briefly describe something you encountered the day before you had this dream.

_____

_____

_____

_____

_____

9. What did you have on your mind before falling asleep on the night you had this dream?

_____

_____

_____

_____

_____

Date: _____ (Enter the date of your dream.)

1. Name the dream: _____ *(This name will typically be the theme or idea of the dream)*

2. How did you feel? _____ *(Afraid, happy, lost, confused, happy, angry, etc.)*

3. Describe the theme *(What was happening, i.e., on the beach, fighting, running, at a party, Day or night, sunny, raining, etc).*

_____

_____

_____

_____

_____

4. List every symbol *(Sofa, water, pool, shoe, dirt, car, truck, dog, mom, dad, sister, etc.)*

A._____   B._____

C._____   D._____

E._____   F._____

G._____   H._____

5. Describe the dream in detail, including its conclusion *(List every color and number that you remember)*

_____

_____

_____

_____

_____

6. Name and describe the individuals in your dream. *(If you do not know the person, state their role in your dream.)*

Their role in the dream   Who are they to you?

A. _____   _____

B. _____   _____

C. _____   _____

D. _____   _____

7. Describe any project(s) you are currently working on?

_____

_____

_____

_____

_____

8. Briefly describe something you encountered the day before you had this dream.

_____

_____

_____

_____

_____

9. What did you have on your mind before falling asleep on the night you had this dream?

_____

_____

_____

_____

_____

https://shifttothereal.com/idreammagus/

Date: _____ (Enter the date of your dream.)

1. Name the dream: _____ *(This name will typically be the theme or idea of the dream)*

2. How did you feel? _____ *(Afraid, happy, lost, confused, happy, angry, etc.)*

3. Describe the theme *(What was happening, i.e., on the beach, fighting, running, at a party, Day or night, sunny, raining, etc).*

_____

_____

_____

_____

_____

4. List every symbol *(Sofa, water, pool, shoe, dirt, car, truck, dog, mom, dad, sister, etc.)*

A._____   B._____

C._____   D._____

E._____   F._____

G._____   H._____

5. Describe the dream in detail, including its conclusion *(List every color and number that you remember)*

_____

_____

_____

_____

_____

6. Name and describe the individuals in your dream. *(If you do not know the person, state their role in your dream.)*

Their role in the dream   Who are they to you?

A. _____   _____

B. _____   _____

C. _____   _____

D. _____   _____

7. Describe any project(s) you are currently working on?

_____

_____

_____

_____

_____

8. Briefly describe something you encountered the day before you had this dream.

_____

_____

_____

_____

_____

9. What did you have on your mind before falling asleep on the night you had this dream?

_____

_____

_____

_____

_____

https://shifttothereal.com/idreammagus/

Date: _____ (Enter the date of your dream.)

1. Name the dream: _____ *(This name will typically be the theme or idea of the dream)*

2. How did you feel? _____ *(Afraid, happy, lost, confused, happy, angry, etc.)*

3. Describe the theme *(What was happening, i.e., on the beach, fighting, running, at a party, Day or night, sunny, raining, etc).*

_____

_____

_____

_____

_____

4. List every symbol *(Sofa, water, pool, shoe, dirt, car, truck, dog, mom, dad, sister, etc.)*

A._____   B._____

C._____   D._____

E._____   F._____

G._____   H._____

5. Describe the dream in detail, including its conclusion *(List every color and number that you remember)*

_____

_____

_____

_____

_____

6. Name and describe the individuals in your dream. *(If you do not know the person, state their role in your dream.)*

          Their role in the dream   Who are they to you?

A. _____   _____

B. _____   _____

C. _____   _____

D. _____   _____

7. Describe any project(s) you are currently working on?

_____

_____

_____

_____

_____

8. Briefly describe something you encountered the day before you had this dream.

_____

_____

_____

_____

_____

9. What did you have on your mind before falling asleep on the night you had this dream?

_____

_____

_____

_____

_____

https://shifttothereal.com/idreammagus/

Date: _____ (Enter the date of your dream.)

1. Name the dream: _____ *(This name will typically be the theme or idea of the dream)*

2. How did you feel? _____ *(Afraid, happy, lost, confused, happy, angry, etc.)*

3. Describe the theme *(What was happening, i.e., on the beach, fighting, running, at a party, Day or night, sunny, raining, etc).*

_____

_____

_____

_____

_____

4. List every symbol *(Sofa, water, pool, shoe, dirt, car, truck, dog, mom, dad, sister, etc.)*

A._____   B._____

C._____   D._____

E._____   F._____

G._____   H._____

5. Describe the dream in detail, including its conclusion *(List every color and number that you remember)*

_____

_____

_____

_____

_____

6. Name and describe the individuals in your dream. *(If you do not know the person, state their role in your dream.)*

            Their role in the dream   Who are they to you?

A. _____   _____

B. _____   _____

C. _____   _____

D. _____   _____

7. Describe any project(s) you are currently working on?

_____

_____

_____

_____

_____

8. Briefly describe something you encountered the day before you had this dream.

_____

_____

_____

_____

_____

9. What did you have on your mind before falling asleep on the night you had this dream?

_____

_____

_____

_____

_____

                         https://shifttothereal.com/idreammagus/

Date: _____ (Enter the date of your dream.)

1. Name the dream: _____ *(This name will typically be the theme or idea of the dream)*

2. How did you feel? _____ *(Afraid, happy, lost, confused, happy, angry, etc.)*

3. Describe the theme *(What was happening, i.e., on the beach, fighting, running, at a party, Day or night, sunny, raining, etc).*

_____

_____

_____

_____

4. List every symbol *(Sofa, water, pool, shoe, dirt, car, truck, dog, mom, dad, sister, etc.)*

A._____   B._____

C._____   D._____

E._____   F._____

G._____   H._____

5. Describe the dream in detail, including its conclusion *(List every color and number that you remember)*

_____

_____

_____

_____

_____

6. Name and describe the individuals in your dream. *(If you do not know the person, state their role in your dream.)*

Their role in the dream   Who are they to you?

A. _____   _____

B. _____   _____

C. _____   _____

D. _____   _____

7. Describe any project(s) you are currently working on?

_____

_____

_____

_____

_____

8. Briefly describe something you encountered the day before you had this dream.

_____

_____

_____

_____

_____

9. What did you have on your mind before falling asleep on the night you had this dream?

_____

_____

_____

_____

_____

https://shifttothereal.com/idreammagus/

Date: _____ (Enter the date of your dream.)

1. Name the dream: _____ *(This name will typically be the theme or idea of the dream)*

2. How did you feel? _____ *(Afraid, happy, lost, confused, happy, angry, etc.)*

3. Describe the theme *(What was happening, i.e., on the beach, fighting, running, at a party, Day or night, sunny, raining, etc).*

_____

_____

_____

_____

_____

4. List every symbol *(Sofa, water, pool, shoe, dirt, car, truck, dog, mom, dad, sister, etc.)*

A._____   B._____

C._____   D._____

E._____   F._____

G._____   H._____

5. Describe the dream in detail, including its conclusion *(List every color and number that you remember)*

_____

_____

_____

_____

_____

6. Name and describe the individuals in your dream. *(If you do not know the person, state their role in your dream.)*

           Their role in the dream   Who are they to you?

A. _____   _____

B. _____   _____

C. _____   _____

D. _____   _____

7. Describe any project(s) you are currently working on?

_____

_____

_____

_____

_____

8. Briefly describe something you encountered the day before you had this dream.

_____

_____

_____

_____

_____

9. What did you have on your mind before falling asleep on the night you had this dream?

_____

_____

_____

_____

_____

Date: _____ (Enter the date of your dream.)

1. Name the dream: _____ *(This name will typically be the theme or idea of the dream)*

2. How did you feel? _____ *(Afraid, happy, lost, confused, happy, angry, etc.)*

3. Describe the theme *(What was happening, i.e., on the beach, fighting, running, at a party, Day or night, sunny, raining, etc).*

_____

_____

_____

_____

_____

4. List every symbol *(Sofa, water, pool, shoe, dirt, car, truck, dog, mom, dad, sister, etc.)*

A._____   B._____

C._____   D._____

E._____   F._____

G._____   H._____

5. Describe the dream in detail, including its conclusion *(List every color and number that you remember)*

_____

_____

_____

_____

_____

6. Name and describe the individuals in your dream. *(If you do not know the person, state their role in your dream.)*

        Their role in the dream   Who are they to you?

A. _____   _____

B. _____   _____

C. _____   _____

D. _____   _____

7. Describe any project(s) you are currently working on?

8. Briefly describe something you encountered the day before you had this dream.

9. What did you have on your mind before falling asleep on the night you had this dream?

Date: _____ (Enter the date of your dream.)

1. Name the dream: _____ *(This name will typically be the theme or idea of the dream)*

2. How did you feel? _____ *(Afraid, happy, lost, confused, happy, angry, etc.)*

3. Describe the theme *(What was happening, i.e., on the beach, fighting, running, at a party, Day or night, sunny, raining, etc).*

_____

_____

_____

_____

_____

4. List every symbol *(Sofa, water, pool, shoe, dirt, car, truck, dog, mom, dad, sister, etc.)*

A._____   B._____

C._____   D._____

E._____   F._____

G._____   H._____

5. Describe the dream in detail, including its conclusion *(List every color and number that you remember)*

_____

_____

_____

_____

_____

6. Name and describe the individuals in your dream. *(If you do not know the person, state their role in your dream.)*

                Their role in the dream   Who are they to you?

    A. _____   _____

    B. _____   _____

    C. _____   _____

    D. _____   _____

7. Describe any project(s) you are currently working on?

_____

_____

_____

_____

_____

8. Briefly describe something you encountered the day before you had this dream.

_____

_____

_____

_____

_____

9. What did you have on your mind before falling asleep on the night you had this dream?

_____

_____

_____

_____

_____

Date: _____ (Enter the date of your dream.)

1. Name the dream: _____ *(This name will typically be the theme or idea of the dream)*

2. How did you feel? _____ *(Afraid, happy, lost, confused, happy, angry, etc.)*

3. Describe the theme *(What was happening, i.e., on the beach, fighting, running, at a party, Day or night, sunny, raining, etc).*

_____

_____

_____

_____

_____

4. List every symbol *(Sofa, water, pool, shoe, dirt, car, truck, dog, mom, dad, sister, etc.)*

A._____   B._____

C._____   D._____

E._____   F._____

G._____   H._____

5. Describe the dream in detail, including its conclusion *(List every color and number that you remember)*

_____

_____

_____

_____

_____

6. Name and describe the individuals in your dream. *(If you do not know the person, state their role in your dream.)*

Their role in the dream	Who are they to you?
A. _____	_____
B. _____	_____
C. _____	_____
D. _____	_____

7. Describe any project(s) you are currently working on?

_____

_____

_____

_____

_____

8. Briefly describe something you encountered the day before you had this dream.

_____

_____

_____

_____

_____

9. What did you have on your mind before falling asleep on the night you had this dream?

_____

_____

_____

_____

_____

https://shifttothereal.com/idreammagus/

Date: _____ (Enter the date of your dream.)

1. Name the dream: _____ *(This name will typically be the theme or idea of the dream)*

2. How did you feel? _____ *(Afraid, happy, lost, confused, happy, angry, etc.)*

3. Describe the theme *(What was happening, i.e., on the beach, fighting, running, at a party, Day or night, sunny, raining, etc).*

_____

_____

_____

_____

_____

4. List every symbol *(Sofa, water, pool, shoe, dirt, car, truck, dog, mom, dad, sister, etc.)*

A._____   B._____

C._____   D._____

E._____   F._____

G._____   H._____

5. Describe the dream in detail, including its conclusion *(List every color and number that you remember)*

_____

_____

_____

_____

_____

6. Name and describe the individuals in your dream. *(If you do not know the person, state their role in your dream.)*

       Their role in the dream   Who are they to you?

A. _____   _____

B. _____   _____

C. _____   _____

D. _____   _____

7. Describe any project(s) you are currently working on?

_____

_____

_____

_____

_____

8. Briefly describe something you encountered the day before you had this dream.

_____

_____

_____

_____

_____

9. What did you have on your mind before falling asleep on the night you had this dream?

_____

_____

_____

_____

_____

Date: _____ (Enter the date of your dream.)

1. Name the dream: _____ *(This name will typically be the theme or idea of the dream)*

2. How did you feel? _____ *(Afraid, happy, lost, confused, happy, angry, etc.)*

3. Describe the theme *(What was happening, i.e., on the beach, fighting, running, at a party, Day or night, sunny, raining, etc).*

_____

_____

_____

_____

_____

4. List every symbol *(Sofa, water, pool, shoe, dirt, car, truck, dog, mom, dad, sister, etc.)*

A._____   B._____

C._____   D._____

E._____   F._____

G._____   H._____

5. Describe the dream in detail, including its conclusion *(List every color and number that you remember)*

_____

_____

_____

_____

_____

6. Name and describe the individuals in your dream. *(If you do not know the person, state their role in your dream.)*

Their role in the dream   Who are they to you?

A. _____   _____

B. _____   _____

C. _____   _____

D. _____   _____

7. Describe any project(s) you are currently working on?

_____

_____

_____

_____

_____

8. Briefly describe something you encountered the day before you had this dream.

_____

_____

_____

_____

_____

9. What did you have on your mind before falling asleep on the night you had this dream?

_____

_____

_____

_____

_____

https://shifttothereal.com/idreammagus/

Date: _____ (Enter the date of your dream.)

1. Name the dream: _____ *(This name will typically be the theme or idea of the dream)*

2. How did you feel? _____ *(Afraid, happy, lost, confused, happy, angry, etc.)*

3. Describe the theme *(What was happening, i.e., on the beach, fighting, running, at a party, Day or night, sunny, raining, etc).*

_____

_____

_____

_____

_____

4. List every symbol *(Sofa, water, pool, shoe, dirt, car, truck, dog, mom, dad, sister, etc.)*

A._____   B._____

C._____   D._____

E._____   F._____

G._____   H._____

5. Describe the dream in detail, including its conclusion *(List every color and number that you remember)*

_____

_____

_____

_____

_____

6. Name and describe the individuals in your dream. *(If you do not know the person, state their role in your dream.)*

Their role in the dream   Who are they to you?

A. _____   _____

B. _____   _____

C. _____   _____

D. _____   _____

7. Describe any project(s) you are currently working on?

_____

_____

_____

_____

_____

8. Briefly describe something you encountered the day before you had this dream.

_____

_____

_____

_____

9. What did you have on your mind before falling asleep on the night you had this dream?

_____

_____

_____

_____

_____

https://shifttothereal.com/idreammagus/

Date: _____ (Enter the date of your dream.)

1. Name the dream: _____ *(This name will typically be the theme or idea of the dream)*

2. How did you feel? _____ *(Afraid, happy, lost, confused, happy, angry, etc.)*

3. Describe the theme *(What was happening, i.e., on the beach, fighting, running, at a party, Day or night, sunny, raining, etc).*

_____

_____

_____

_____

_____

4. List every symbol *(Sofa, water, pool, shoe, dirt, car, truck, dog, mom, dad, sister, etc.)*

A._____   B._____

C._____   D._____

E._____   F._____

G._____   H._____

5. Describe the dream in detail, including its conclusion *(List every color and number that you remember)*

_____

_____

_____

_____

_____

6. Name and describe the individuals in your dream. *(If you do not know the person, state their role in your dream.)*

Their role in the dream	Who are they to you?
A. _____	_____
B. _____	_____
C. _____	_____
D. _____	_____

7. Describe any project(s) you are currently working on?

_____

_____

_____

_____

_____

8. Briefly describe something you encountered the day before you had this dream.

_____

_____

_____

_____

_____

9. What did you have on your mind before falling asleep on the night you had this dream?

_____

_____

_____

_____

https://shifttothereal.com/idreammagus/

Date: _____ (Enter the date of your dream.)

1. Name the dream: _____ *(This name will typically be the theme or idea of the dream)*

2. How did you feel? _____ *(Afraid, happy, lost, confused, happy, angry, etc.)*

3. Describe the theme *(What was happening, i.e., on the beach, fighting, running, at a party, Day or night, sunny, raining, etc).*

_____

_____

_____

_____

_____

4. List every symbol *(Sofa, water, pool, shoe, dirt, car, truck, dog, mom, dad, sister, etc.)*

A._____   B._____

C._____   D._____

E._____   F._____

G._____   H._____

5. Describe the dream in detail, including its conclusion *(List every color and number that you remember)*

_____

_____

_____

_____

_____

6. Name and describe the individuals in your dream. *(If you do not know the person, state their role in your dream.)*

Their role in the dream   Who are they to you?

A. _____   _____

B. _____   _____

C. _____   _____

D. _____   _____

7. Describe any project(s) you are currently working on?

_____

_____

_____

_____

_____

8. Briefly describe something you encountered the day before you had this dream.

_____

_____

_____

_____

_____

9. What did you have on your mind before falling asleep on the night you had this dream?

_____

_____

_____

_____

_____

https://shifttothereal.com/idreammagus/

Date: _____ (Enter the date of your dream.)

1. Name the dream: _____ *(This name will typically be the theme or idea of the dream)*

2. How did you feel? _____ *(Afraid, happy, lost, confused, happy, angry, etc.)*

3. Describe the theme *(What was happening, i.e., on the beach, fighting, running, at a party, Day or night, sunny, raining, etc).*

_____

_____

_____

_____

_____

4. List every symbol *(Sofa, water, pool, shoe, dirt, car, truck, dog, mom, dad, sister, etc.)*

A._____   B._____

C._____   D._____

E._____   F._____

G._____   H._____

5. Describe the dream in detail, including its conclusion *(List every color and number that you remember)*

_____

_____

_____

_____

_____

6. Name and describe the individuals in your dream. *(If you do not know the person, state their role in your dream.)*

   Their role in the dream   Who are they to you?

   A. _____   _____

   B. _____   _____

   C. _____   _____

   D. _____   _____

7. Describe any project(s) you are currently working on?

_____

_____

_____

_____

_____

8. Briefly describe something you encountered the day before you had this dream.

_____

_____

_____

_____

_____

9. What did you have on your mind before falling asleep on the night you had this dream?

_____

_____

_____

_____

_____

https://shifttothereal.com/idreammagus/

Date: _____ (Enter the date of your dream.)

1. Name the dream: _____ *(This name will typically be the theme or idea of the dream)*

2. How did you feel? _____ *(Afraid, happy, lost, confused, happy, angry, etc.)*

3. Describe the theme *(What was happening, i.e., on the beach, fighting, running, at a party, Day or night, sunny, raining, etc).*

_____

_____

_____

_____

_____

4. List every symbol *(Sofa, water, pool, shoe, dirt, car, truck, dog, mom, dad, sister, etc.)*

A._____   B._____

C._____   D._____

E._____   F._____

G._____   H._____

5. Describe the dream in detail, including its conclusion *(List every color and number that you remember)*

_____

_____

_____

_____

_____

6. Name and describe the individuals in your dream. *(If you do not know the person, state their role in your dream.)*

Their role in the dream   Who are they to you?

A. _____   _____

B. _____   _____

C. _____   _____

D. _____   _____

7. Describe any project(s) you are currently working on?

_____

_____

_____

_____

_____

8. Briefly describe something you encountered the day before you had this dream.

_____

_____

_____

_____

_____

9. What did you have on your mind before falling asleep on the night you had this dream?

_____

_____

_____

_____

_____

Date: _____ (Enter the date of your dream.)

1. Name the dream: _____ (This name will typically be the theme or idea of the dream)

2. How did you feel? _____ (Afraid, happy, lost, confused, happy, angry, etc.)

3. Describe the theme (What was happening, i.e., on the beach, fighting, running, at a party, Day or night, sunny, raining, etc).

_____

_____

_____

_____

_____

4. List every symbol (Sofa, water, pool, shoe, dirt, car, truck, dog, mom, dad, sister, etc.)

A._____   B._____

C._____   D._____

E._____   F._____

G._____   H._____

5. Describe the dream in detail, including its conclusion (List every color and number that you remember)

_____

_____

_____

_____

_____

6. Name and describe the individuals in your dream. *(If you do not know the person, state their role in your dream.)*

Their role in the dream	Who are they to you?
A. _____	_____
B. _____	_____
C. _____	_____
D. _____	_____

7. Describe any project(s) you are currently working on?

_____

_____

_____

_____

_____

8. Briefly describe something you encountered the day before you had this dream.

_____

_____

_____

_____

_____

9. What did you have on your mind before falling asleep on the night you had this dream?

_____

_____

_____

_____

_____

https://shifttothereal.com/idreammagus/

Date: _____ (Enter the date of your dream.)

1. Name the dream: _____ *(This name will typically be the theme or idea of the dream)*

2. How did you feel? _____ *(Afraid, happy, lost, confused, happy, angry, etc.)*

3. Describe the theme *(What was happening, i.e., on the beach, fighting, running, at a party, Day or night, sunny, raining, etc).*

_____

_____

_____

_____

_____

4. List every symbol *(Sofa, water, pool, shoe, dirt, car, truck, dog, mom, dad, sister, etc.)*

A._____   B._____

C._____   D._____

E._____   F._____

G._____   H._____

5. Describe the dream in detail, including its conclusion *(List every color and number that you remember)*

_____

_____

_____

_____

_____

6. Name and describe the individuals in your dream. *(If you do not know the person, state their role in your dream.)*

Their role in the dream   Who are they to you?

A. _____   _____

B. _____   _____

C. _____   _____

D. _____   _____

7. Describe any project(s) you are currently working on?

_____

_____

_____

_____

_____

8. Briefly describe something you encountered the day before you had this dream.

_____

_____

_____

_____

_____

9. What did you have on your mind before falling asleep on the night you had this dream?

_____

_____

_____

_____

_____

https://shifttothereal.com/idreammagus/

Date: _____ (Enter the date of your dream.)

1. Name the dream: _____ *(This name will typically be the theme or idea of the dream)*

2. How did you feel? _____ *(Afraid, happy, lost, confused, happy, angry, etc.)*

3. Describe the theme *(What was happening, i.e., on the beach, fighting, running, at a party, Day or night, sunny, raining, etc).*

_____

_____

_____

_____

_____

4. List every symbol *(Sofa, water, pool, shoe, dirt, car, truck, dog, mom, dad, sister, etc.)*

A._____   B._____

C._____   D._____

E._____   F._____

G._____   H._____

5. Describe the dream in detail, including its conclusion *(List every color and number that you remember)*

_____

_____

_____

_____

_____

6. Name and describe the individuals in your dream. *(If you do not know the person, state their role in your dream.)*

Their role in the dream   Who are they to you?

A. _____   _____

B. _____   _____

C. _____   _____

D. _____   _____

7. Describe any project(s) you are currently working on?

_____

_____

_____

_____

_____

8. Briefly describe something you encountered the day before you had this dream.

_____

_____

_____

_____

_____

9. What did you have on your mind before falling asleep on the night you had this dream?

_____

_____

_____

_____

_____

https://shifttothereal.com/idreammagus/

Date: _____ (Enter the date of your dream.)

1. Name the dream: _____ *(This name will typically be the theme or idea of the dream)*

2. How did you feel? _____ *(Afraid, happy, lost, confused, happy, angry, etc.)*

3. Describe the theme *(What was happening, i.e., on the beach, fighting, running, at a party, Day or night, sunny, raining, etc).*

_____

_____

_____

_____

_____

4. List every symbol *(Sofa, water, pool, shoe, dirt, car, truck, dog, mom, dad, sister, etc.)*

A._____   B._____

C._____   D._____

E._____   F._____

G._____   H._____

5. Describe the dream in detail, including its conclusion *(List every color and number that you remember)*

_____

_____

_____

_____

_____

6. Name and describe the individuals in your dream. *(If you do not know the person, state their role in your dream.)*

   Their role in the dream   Who are they to you?

   A. _____   _____

   B. _____   _____

   C. _____   _____

   D. _____   _____

7. Describe any project(s) you are currently working on?

   _____

   _____

   _____

   _____

   _____

8. Briefly describe something you encountered the day before you had this dream.

   _____

   _____

   _____

   _____

   _____

9. What did you have on your mind before falling asleep on the night you had this dream?

   _____

   _____

   _____

   _____

   _____

Date: _____ (Enter the date of your dream.)

1. Name the dream: _____ *(This name will typically be the theme or idea of the dream)*

2. How did you feel? _____ *(Afraid, happy, lost, confused, happy, angry, etc.)*

3. Describe the theme *(What was happening, i.e., on the beach, fighting, running, at a party, Day or night, sunny, raining, etc).*

_____

_____

_____

_____

_____

4. List every symbol *(Sofa, water, pool, shoe, dirt, car, truck, dog, mom, dad, sister, etc.)*

A._____   B._____

C._____   D._____

E._____   F._____

G._____   H._____

5. Describe the dream in detail, including its conclusion *(List every color and number that you remember)*

_____

_____

_____

_____

_____

6. Name and describe the individuals in your dream. *(If you do not know the person, state their role in your dream.)*

Their role in the dream	Who are they to you?
A. _____	_____
B. _____	_____
C. _____	_____
D. _____	_____

7. Describe any project(s) you are currently working on?

_____

_____

_____

_____

_____

8. Briefly describe something you encountered the day before you had this dream.

_____

_____

_____

_____

_____

9. What did you have on your mind before falling asleep on the night you had this dream?

_____

_____

_____

_____

_____

Date: _____ (Enter the date of your dream.)

1. Name the dream: _____ *(This name will typically be the theme or idea of the dream)*

2. How did you feel? _____ *(Afraid, happy, lost, confused, happy, angry, etc.)*

3. Describe the theme *(What was happening, i.e., on the beach, fighting, running, at a party, Day or night, sunny, raining, etc).*

_____

_____

_____

_____

_____

4. List every symbol *(Sofa, water, pool, shoe, dirt, car, truck, dog, mom, dad, sister, etc.)*

A._____ B._____

C._____ D._____

E._____ F._____

G._____ H._____

5. Describe the dream in detail, including its conclusion *(List every color and number that you remember)*

_____

_____

_____

_____

_____

6. Name and describe the individuals in your dream. *(If you do not know the person, state their role in your dream.)*

Their role in the dream   Who are they to you?

A. _____   _____

B. _____   _____

C. _____   _____

D. _____   _____

7. Describe any project(s) you are currently working on?

_____

_____

_____

_____

_____

8. Briefly describe something you encountered the day before you had this dream.

_____

_____

_____

_____

_____

9. What did you have on your mind before falling asleep on the night you had this dream?

_____

_____

_____

_____

_____

Date: _____ (Enter the date of your dream.)

1. Name the dream: _____ *(This name will typically be the theme or idea of the dream)*

2. How did you feel? _____ *(Afraid, happy, lost, confused, happy, angry, etc.)*

3. Describe the theme *(What was happening, i.e., on the beach, fighting, running, at a party, Day or night, sunny, raining, etc).*

_____

_____

_____

_____

_____

4. List every symbol *(Sofa, water, pool, shoe, dirt, car, truck, dog, mom, dad, sister, etc.)*

A._____   B._____

C._____   D._____

E._____   F._____

G._____   H._____

5. Describe the dream in detail, including its conclusion *(List every color and number that you remember)*

_____

_____

_____

_____

_____

6. Name and describe the individuals in your dream. *(If you do not know the person, state their role in your dream.)*

Their role in the dream   Who are they to you?

A. _____   _____

B. _____   _____

C. _____   _____

D. _____   _____

7. Describe any project(s) you are currently working on?

_____

_____

_____

_____

_____

8. Briefly describe something you encountered the day before you had this dream.

_____

_____

_____

_____

_____

9. What did you have on your mind before falling asleep on the night you had this dream?

_____

_____

_____

_____

_____

https://shifttothereal.com/idreammagus/

Date: _____ (Enter the date of your dream.)

1. Name the dream: _____ *(This name will typically be the theme or idea of the dream)*

2. How did you feel? _____ *(Afraid, happy, lost, confused, happy, angry, etc.)*

3. Describe the theme *(What was happening, i.e., on the beach, fighting, running, at a party, Day or night, sunny, raining, etc).*

_____

_____

_____

_____

_____

4. List every symbol *(Sofa, water, pool, shoe, dirt, car, truck, dog, mom, dad, sister, etc.)*

A._____   B._____

C._____   D._____

E._____   F._____

G._____   H._____

5. Describe the dream in detail, including its conclusion *(List every color and number that you remember)*

_____

_____

_____

_____

_____

6. Name and describe the individuals in your dream. *(If you do not know the person, state their role in your dream.)*

Their role in the dream   Who are they to you?

A. _____   _____

B. _____   _____

C. _____   _____

D. _____   _____

7. Describe any project(s) you are currently working on?

_____

_____

_____

_____

_____

8. Briefly describe something you encountered the day before you had this dream.

_____

_____

_____

_____

_____

9. What did you have on your mind before falling asleep on the night you had this dream?

_____

_____

_____

_____

_____

https://shifttothereal.com/idreammagus/

Date: _____ (Enter the date of your dream.)

1. Name the dream: _____ *(This name will typically be the theme or idea of the dream)*

2. How did you feel? _____ *(Afraid, happy, lost, confused, happy, angry, etc.)*

3. Describe the theme *(What was happening, i.e., on the beach, fighting, running, at a party, Day or night, sunny, raining, etc).*

_____

_____

_____

_____

_____

4. List every symbol *(Sofa, water, pool, shoe, dirt, car, truck, dog, mom, dad, sister, etc.)*

A._____   B._____

C._____   D._____

E._____   F._____

G._____   H._____

5. Describe the dream in detail, including its conclusion *(List every color and number that you remember)*

_____

_____

_____

_____

_____

6. Name and describe the individuals in your dream. *(If you do not know the person, state their role in your dream.)*

Their role in the dream   Who are they to you?

A._____   _____

B._____   _____

C._____   _____

D._____   _____

7. Describe any project(s) you are currently working on?

_____

_____

_____

_____

_____

8. Briefly describe something you encountered the day before you had this dream.

_____

_____

_____

_____

_____

9. What did you have on your mind before falling asleep on the night you had this dream?

_____

_____

_____

_____

_____

https://shifttothereal.com/idreammagus/

Date: _____ (Enter the date of your dream.)

1. Name the dream: _____ *(This name will typically be the theme or idea of the dream)*

2. How did you feel? _____ *(Afraid, happy, lost, confused, happy, angry, etc.)*

3. Describe the theme *(What was happening, i.e., on the beach, fighting, running, at a party, Day or night, sunny, raining, etc).*

_____

_____

_____

_____

_____

4. List every symbol *(Sofa, water, pool, shoe, dirt, car, truck, dog, mom, dad, sister, etc.)*

A._____ B._____

C._____ D._____

E._____ F._____

G._____ H._____

5. Describe the dream in detail, including its conclusion *(List every color and number that you remember)*

_____

_____

_____

_____

_____

6. Name and describe the individuals in your dream. *(If you do not know the person, state their role in your dream.)*

Their role in the dream   Who are they to you?

A. _____   _____

B. _____   _____

C. _____   _____

D. _____   _____

7. Describe any project(s) you are currently working on?

_____

_____

_____

_____

_____

8. Briefly describe something you encountered the day before you had this dream.

_____

_____

_____

_____

_____

9. What did you have on your mind before falling asleep on the night you had this dream?

_____

_____

_____

_____

_____

Date: _____ (Enter the date of your dream.)

1. Name the dream: _____ *(This name will typically be the theme or idea of the dream)*

2. How did you feel? _____ *(Afraid, happy, lost, confused, happy, angry, etc.)*

3. Describe the theme *(What was happening, i.e., on the beach, fighting, running, at a party, Day or night, sunny, raining, etc).*

_____

_____

_____

_____

_____

4. List every symbol *(Sofa, water, pool, shoe, dirt, car, truck, dog, mom, dad, sister, etc.)*

A._____   B._____

C._____   D._____

E._____   F._____

G._____   H._____

5. Describe the dream in detail, including its conclusion *(List every color and number that you remember)*

_____

_____

_____

_____

_____

6. Name and describe the individuals in your dream. *(If you do not know the person, state their role in your dream.)*

Their role in the dream   Who are they to you?

A. _____   _____

B. _____   _____

C. _____   _____

D. _____   _____

7. Describe any project(s) you are currently working on?

_____

_____

_____

_____

_____

8. Briefly describe something you encountered the day before you had this dream.

_____

_____

_____

_____

_____

9. What did you have on your mind before falling asleep on the night you had this dream?

_____

_____

_____

_____

_____

Date: _____ (Enter the date of your dream.)

1. Name the dream: _____ *(This name will typically be the theme or idea of the dream)*

2. How did you feel? _____ *(Afraid, happy, lost, confused, happy, angry, etc.)*

3. Describe the theme *(What was happening, i.e., on the beach, fighting, running, at a party, Day or night, sunny, raining, etc).*

_____

_____

_____

_____

_____

4. List every symbol *(Sofa, water, pool, shoe, dirt, car, truck, dog, mom, dad, sister, etc.)*

A._____   B._____

C._____   D._____

E._____   F._____

G._____   H._____

5. Describe the dream in detail, including its conclusion *(List every color and number that you remember)*

_____

_____

_____

_____

_____

6. Name and describe the individuals in your dream. *(If you do not know the person, state their role in your dream.)*

Their role in the dream   Who are they to you?

A. _____   _____

B. _____   _____

C. _____   _____

D. _____   _____

7. Describe any project(s) you are currently working on?

_____

_____

_____

_____

_____

8. Briefly describe something you encountered the day before you had this dream.

_____

_____

_____

_____

_____

9. What did you have on your mind before falling asleep on the night you had this dream?

_____

_____

_____

_____

_____

Date: _____ (Enter the date of your dream.)

1. Name the dream: _____ (*This name will typically be the theme or idea of the dream*)

2. How did you feel? _____ (*Afraid, happy, lost, confused, happy, angry, etc.*)

3. Describe the theme (*What was happening, i.e., on the beach, fighting, running, at a party, Day or night, sunny, raining, etc*).

_____

_____

_____

_____

_____

4. List every symbol (*Sofa, water, pool, shoe, dirt, car, truck, dog, mom, dad, sister, etc.*)

A._____   B._____

C._____   D._____

E._____   F._____

G._____   H._____

5. Describe the dream in detail, including its conclusion (*List every color and number that you remember*)

_____

_____

_____

_____

_____

6. Name and describe the individuals in your dream. *(If you do not know the person, state their role in your dream.)*

Their role in the dream   Who are they to you?

A. _____   _____

B. _____   _____

C. _____   _____

D. _____   _____

7. Describe any project(s) you are currently working on?

_____

_____

_____

_____

_____

8. Briefly describe something you encountered the day before you had this dream.

_____

_____

_____

_____

_____

_____

9. What did you have on your mind before falling asleep on the night you had this dream?

_____

_____

_____

_____

_____

https://shifttothereal.com/idreammagus/

Date: _____ (Enter the date of your dream.)

1. Name the dream: _____ *(This name will typically be the theme or idea of the dream)*

2. How did you feel? _____ *(Afraid, happy, lost, confused, happy, angry, etc.)*

3. Describe the theme *(What was happening, i.e., on the beach, fighting, running, at a party, Day or night, sunny, raining, etc).*

_____

_____

_____

_____

_____

4. List every symbol *(Sofa, water, pool, shoe, dirt, car, truck, dog, mom, dad, sister, etc.)*

A._____   B._____

C._____   D._____

E._____   F._____

G._____   H._____

5. Describe the dream in detail, including its conclusion *(List every color and number that you remember)*

_____

_____

_____

_____

_____

6. Name and describe the individuals in your dream. *(If you do not know the person, state their role in your dream.)*

Their role in the dream	Who are they to you?
A. _____	_____
B. _____	_____
C. _____	_____
D. _____	_____

7. Describe any project(s) you are currently working on?

_____

_____

_____

_____

_____

8. Briefly describe something you encountered the day before you had this dream.

_____

_____

_____

_____

_____

9. What did you have on your mind before falling asleep on the night you had this dream?

_____

_____

_____

_____

_____

https://shifttothereal.com/idreammagus/

Date: _____ (Enter the date of your dream.)

1. Name the dream: _____ *(This name will typically be the theme or idea of the dream)*

2. How did you feel? _____ *(Afraid, happy, lost, confused, happy, angry, etc.)*

3. Describe the theme *(What was happening, i.e., on the beach, fighting, running, at a party, Day or night, sunny, raining, etc).*

_____

_____

_____

_____

_____

4. List every symbol *(Sofa, water, pool, shoe, dirt, car, truck, dog, mom, dad, sister, etc.)*

A._____   B._____

C._____   D._____

E._____   F._____

G._____   H._____

5. Describe the dream in detail, including its conclusion *(List every color and number that you remember)*

_____

_____

_____

_____

_____

6. Name and describe the individuals in your dream. *(If you do not know the person, state their role in your dream.)*

          Their role in the dream   Who are they to you?

A. _____   _____

B. _____   _____

C. _____   _____

D. _____   _____

7. Describe any project(s) you are currently working on?

_____

_____

_____

_____

_____

8. Briefly describe something you encountered the day before you had this dream.

_____

_____

_____

_____

_____

9. What did you have on your mind before falling asleep on the night you had this dream?

_____

_____

_____

_____

_____

https://shifttothereal.com/idreammagus/

Date: _____ (Enter the date of your dream.)

1. Name the dream: _____ *(This name will typically be the theme or idea of the dream)*

2. How did you feel? _____ *(Afraid, happy, lost, confused, happy, angry, etc.)*

3. Describe the theme *(What was happening, i.e., on the beach, fighting, running, at a party, Day or night, sunny, raining, etc).*

_____
_____
_____
_____
_____

4. List every symbol *(Sofa, water, pool, shoe, dirt, car, truck, dog, mom, dad, sister, etc.)*

A._____   B._____
C._____   D._____
E._____   F._____
G._____   H._____

5. Describe the dream in detail, including its conclusion *(List every color and number that you remember)*

_____
_____
_____
_____
_____

6. Name and describe the individuals in your dream. *(If you do not know the person, state their role in your dream.)*

       Their role in the dream   Who are they to you?

A. _____   _____

B. _____   _____

C. _____   _____

D. _____   _____

7. Describe any project(s) you are currently working on?

8. Briefly describe something you encountered the day before you had this dream.

9. What did you have on your mind before falling asleep on the night you had this dream?

Date: _____ (Enter the date of your dream.)

1. Name the dream: _____ *(This name will typically be the theme or idea of the dream)*

2. How did you feel? _____ *(Afraid, happy, lost, confused, happy, angry, etc.)*

3. Describe the theme *(What was happening, i.e., on the beach, fighting, running, at a party, Day or night, sunny, raining, etc).*

_____

_____

_____

_____

_____

4. List every symbol *(Sofa, water, pool, shoe, dirt, car, truck, dog, mom, dad, sister, etc.)*

A._____   B._____

C._____   D._____

E._____   F._____

G._____   H._____

5. Describe the dream in detail, including its conclusion *(List every color and number that you remember)*

_____

_____

_____

_____

_____

6. Name and describe the individuals in your dream. *(If you do not know the person, state their role in your dream.)*

Their role in the dream　　　　　　Who are they to you?

A. _____　　_____

B. _____　　_____

C. _____　　_____

D. _____　　_____

7. Describe any project(s) you are currently working on?

_____

_____

_____

_____

_____

8. Briefly describe something you encountered the day before you had this dream.

_____

_____

_____

_____

_____

9. What did you have on your mind before falling asleep on the night you had this dream?

_____

_____

_____

_____

　　　　　　　　https://shifttothereal.com/idreammagus/

Date: _____ (Enter the date of your dream.)

1. Name the dream: _____ *(This name will typically be the theme or idea of the dream)*

2. How did you feel? _____ *(Afraid, happy, lost, confused, happy, angry, etc.)*

3. Describe the theme *(What was happening, i.e., on the beach, fighting, running, at a party, Day or night, sunny, raining, etc).*

_____

_____

_____

_____

_____

4. List every symbol *(Sofa, water, pool, shoe, dirt, car, truck, dog, mom, dad, sister, etc.)*

A._____   B._____

C._____   D._____

E._____   F._____

G._____   H._____

5. Describe the dream in detail, including its conclusion *(List every color and number that you remember)*

_____

_____

_____

_____

_____

6. Name and describe the individuals in your dream. *(If you do not know the person, state their role in your dream.)*

Their role in the dream   Who are they to you?

A. _____   _____

B. _____   _____

C. _____   _____

D. _____   _____

7. Describe any project(s) you are currently working on?

_____

_____

_____

_____

_____

8. Briefly describe something you encountered the day before you had this dream.

_____

_____

_____

_____

_____

9. What did you have on your mind before falling asleep on the night you had this dream?

_____

_____

_____

_____

_____

                    https://shifttothereal.com/idreammagus/

Date: _____ (Enter the date of your dream.)

1. Name the dream: _____ *(This name will typically be the theme or idea of the dream)*

2. How did you feel? _____ *(Afraid, happy, lost, confused, happy, angry, etc.)*

3. Describe the theme *(What was happening, i.e., on the beach, fighting, running, at a party, Day or night, sunny, raining, etc).*

_____

_____

_____

_____

_____

4. List every symbol *(Sofa, water, pool, shoe, dirt, car, truck, dog, mom, dad, sister, etc.)*

A._____   B._____

C._____   D._____

E._____   F._____

G._____   H._____

5. Describe the dream in detail, including its conclusion *(List every color and number that you remember)*

_____

_____

_____

_____

_____

6. Name and describe the individuals in your dream. *(If you do not know the person, state their role in your dream.)*

Their role in the dream	Who are they to you?
A. _____	_____
B. _____	_____
C. _____	_____
D. _____	_____

7. Describe any project(s) you are currently working on?

_____

_____

_____

_____

_____

8. Briefly describe something you encountered the day before you had this dream.

_____

_____

_____

_____

_____

9. What did you have on your mind before falling asleep on the night you had this dream?

_____

_____

_____

_____

_____

✷ A DREAM CATCHER'S JOURNAL ✷

Date: _____ (Enter the date of your dream.)

1. Name the dream: _____ *(This name will typically be the theme or idea of the dream)*

2. How did you feel? _____ *(Afraid, happy, lost, confused, happy, angry, etc.)*

3. Describe the theme *(What was happening, i.e., on the beach, fighting, running, at a party, Day or night, sunny, raining, etc).*

_____
_____
_____
_____
_____

4. List every symbol *(Sofa, water, pool, shoe, dirt, car, truck, dog, mom, dad, sister, etc.)*

A._____ B._____
C._____ D._____
E._____ F._____
G._____ H._____

5. Describe the dream in detail, including its conclusion *(List every color and number that you remember)*

_____
_____
_____
_____
_____

6. Name and describe the individuals in your dream. *(If you do not know the person, state their role in your dream.)*

        Their role in the dream   Who are they to you?

    A. _____   _____

    B. _____   _____

    C. _____   _____

    D. _____   _____

7. Describe any project(s) you are currently working on?

_____

_____

_____

_____

_____

8. Briefly describe something you encountered the day before you had this dream.

_____

_____

_____

_____

_____

9. What did you have on your mind before falling asleep on the night you had this dream?

_____

_____

_____

_____

_____

                                           https://shifttothereal.com/idreammagus/

Date: _____ (Enter the date of your dream.)

1. Name the dream: _____ *(This name will typically be the theme or idea of the dream)*

2. How did you feel? _____ *(Afraid, happy, lost, confused, happy, angry, etc.)*

3. Describe the theme *(What was happening, i.e., on the beach, fighting, running, at a party, Day or night, sunny, raining, etc).*

_____

_____

_____

_____

_____

4. List every symbol *(Sofa, water, pool, shoe, dirt, car, truck, dog, mom, dad, sister, etc.)*

A._____   B._____

C._____   D._____

E._____   F._____

G._____   H._____

5. Describe the dream in detail, including its conclusion *(List every color and number that you remember)*

_____

_____

_____

_____

_____

6. Name and describe the individuals in your dream. *(If you do not know the person, state their role in your dream.)*

       Their role in the dream   Who are they to you?

A. _____   _____

B. _____   _____

C. _____   _____

D. _____   _____

7. Describe any project(s) you are currently working on?

_____

_____

_____

_____

_____

8. Briefly describe something you encountered the day before you had this dream.

_____

_____

_____

_____

_____

9. What did you have on your mind before falling asleep on the night you had this dream?

_____

_____

_____

_____

_____

Date: _____ (Enter the date of your dream.)

1. Name the dream: _____ *(This name will typically be the theme or idea of the dream)*

2. How did you feel? _____ *(Afraid, happy, lost, confused, happy, angry, etc.)*

3. Describe the theme *(What was happening, i.e., on the beach, fighting, running, at a party, Day or night, sunny, raining, etc).*

_____

_____

_____

_____

_____

4. List every symbol *(Sofa, water, pool, shoe, dirt, car, truck, dog, mom, dad, sister, etc.)*

A._____   B._____

C._____   D._____

E._____   F._____

G._____   H._____

5. Describe the dream in detail, including its conclusion *(List every color and number that you remember)*

_____

_____

_____

_____

_____

6. Name and describe the individuals in your dream. *(If you do not know the person, state their role in your dream.)*

         Their role in the dream   Who are they to you?

A. _____   _____

B. _____   _____

C. _____   _____

D. _____   _____

7. Describe any project(s) you are currently working on?

_____

_____

_____

_____

_____

8. Briefly describe something you encountered the day before you had this dream.

_____

_____

_____

_____

_____

9. What did you have on your mind before falling asleep on the night you had this dream?

_____

_____

_____

_____

_____

https://shifttothereal.com/idreammagus/

Date: _____ (Enter the date of your dream.)

1. Name the dream: _____ *(This name will typically be the theme or idea of the dream)*

2. How did you feel? _____ *(Afraid, happy, lost, confused, happy, angry, etc.)*

3. Describe the theme *(What was happening, i.e., on the beach, fighting, running, at a party, Day or night, sunny, raining, etc).*

_____

_____

_____

_____

_____

4. List every symbol *(Sofa, water, pool, shoe, dirt, car, truck, dog, mom, dad, sister, etc.)*

A._____   B._____

C._____   D._____

E._____   F._____

G._____   H._____

5. Describe the dream in detail, including its conclusion *(List every color and number that you remember)*

_____

_____

_____

_____

_____

6. Name and describe the individuals in your dream. *(If you do not know the person, state their role in your dream.)*

        Their role in the dream   Who are they to you?

A. _____   _____

B. _____   _____

C. _____   _____

D. _____   _____

7. Describe any project(s) you are currently working on?

_____

_____

_____

_____

_____

8. Briefly describe something you encountered the day before you had this dream.

_____

_____

_____

_____

_____

9. What did you have on your mind before falling asleep on the night you had this dream?

_____

_____

_____

_____

_____

Date: _____ (Enter the date of your dream.)

1. Name the dream: _____ *(This name will typically be the theme or idea of the dream)*

2. How did you feel? _____ *(Afraid, happy, lost, confused, happy, angry, etc.)*

3. Describe the theme *(What was happening, i.e., on the beach, fighting, running, at a party, Day or night, sunny, raining, etc).*

_____

_____

_____

_____

_____

4. List every symbol *(Sofa, water, pool, shoe, dirt, car, truck, dog, mom, dad, sister, etc.)*

A._____   B._____

C._____   D._____

E._____   F._____

G._____   H._____

5. Describe the dream in detail, including its conclusion *(List every color and number that you remember)*

_____

_____

_____

_____

_____

6. Name and describe the individuals in your dream. *(If you do not know the person, state their role in your dream.)*

Their role in the dream   Who are they to you?

A. _____   _____

B. _____   _____

C. _____   _____

D. _____   _____

7. Describe any project(s) you are currently working on?

_____

_____

_____

_____

_____

8. Briefly describe something you encountered the day before you had this dream.

_____

_____

_____

_____

_____

9. What did you have on your mind before falling asleep on the night you had this dream?

_____

_____

_____

_____

_____

Date: _____ (Enter the date of your dream.)

1. Name the dream: _____ *(This name will typically be the theme or idea of the dream)*

2. How did you feel? _____ *(Afraid, happy, lost, confused, happy, angry, etc.)*

3. Describe the theme *(What was happening, i.e., on the beach, fighting, running, at a party, Day or night, sunny, raining, etc).*

_____

_____

_____

_____

_____

4. List every symbol *(Sofa, water, pool, shoe, dirt, car, truck, dog, mom, dad, sister, etc.)*

A._____   B._____

C._____   D._____

E._____   F._____

G._____   H._____

5. Describe the dream in detail, including its conclusion *(List every color and number that you remember)*

_____

_____

_____

_____

_____

6. Name and describe the individuals in your dream. *(If you do not know the person, state their role in your dream.)*

          Their role in the dream   Who are they to you?

    A. _____   _____

    B. _____   _____

    C. _____   _____

    D. _____   _____

7. Describe any project(s) you are currently working on?

_____

_____

_____

_____

_____

8. Briefly describe something you encountered the day before you had this dream.

_____

_____

_____

_____

_____

9. What did you have on your mind before falling asleep on the night you had this dream?

_____

_____

_____

_____

_____

                             https://shifttothereal.com/idreammagus/

Date: _____ (Enter the date of your dream.)

1. Name the dream: _____ *(This name will typically be the theme or idea of the dream)*

2. How did you feel? _____ *(Afraid, happy, lost, confused, happy, angry, etc.)*

3. Describe the theme *(What was happening, i.e., on the beach, fighting, running, at a party, Day or night, sunny, raining, etc).*

_____

_____

_____

_____

_____

4. List every symbol *(Sofa, water, pool, shoe, dirt, car, truck, dog, mom, dad, sister, etc.)*

A._____   B._____

C._____   D._____

E._____   F._____

G._____   H._____

5. Describe the dream in detail, including its conclusion *(List every color and number that you remember)*

_____

_____

_____

_____

_____

6. Name and describe the individuals in your dream. *(If you do not know the person, state their role in your dream.)*

      Their role in the dream   Who are they to you?

A. _____   _____

B. _____   _____

C. _____   _____

D. _____   _____

7. Describe any project(s) you are currently working on?

_____

_____

_____

_____

_____

8. Briefly describe something you encountered the day before you had this dream.

_____

_____

_____

_____

_____

9. What did you have on your mind before falling asleep on the night you had this dream?

_____

_____

_____

_____

_____

https://shifttothereal.com/idreammagus/

Date: _____ (Enter the date of your dream.)

1. Name the dream: _____ *(This name will typically be the theme or idea of the dream)*

2. How did you feel? _____ *(Afraid, happy, lost, confused, happy, angry, etc.)*

3. Describe the theme *(What was happening, i.e., on the beach, fighting, running, at a party, Day or night, sunny, raining, etc).*

_____

_____

_____

_____

_____

4. List every symbol *(Sofa, water, pool, shoe, dirt, car, truck, dog, mom, dad, sister, etc.)*

A._____ B._____

C._____ D._____

E._____ F._____

G._____ H._____

5. Describe the dream in detail, including its conclusion *(List every color and number that you remember)*

_____

_____

_____

_____

_____

6. Name and describe the individuals in your dream. *(If you do not know the person, state their role in your dream.)*

Their role in the dream	Who are they to you?
A. _____	_____
B. _____	_____
C. _____	_____
D. _____	_____

7. Describe any project(s) you are currently working on?

_____

_____

_____

_____

_____

8. Briefly describe something you encountered the day before you had this dream.

_____

_____

_____

_____

_____

9. What did you have on your mind before falling asleep on the night you had this dream?

_____

_____

_____

_____

_____

https://shifttothereal.com/idreammagus/

Date: _____ (Enter the date of your dream.)

1. Name the dream: _____ *(This name will typically be the theme or idea of the dream)*

2. How did you feel? _____ *(Afraid, happy, lost, confused, happy, angry, etc.)*

3. Describe the theme *(What was happening, i.e., on the beach, fighting, running, at a party, Day or night, sunny, raining, etc).*

_____

_____

_____

_____

_____

4. List every symbol *(Sofa, water, pool, shoe, dirt, car, truck, dog, mom, dad, sister, etc.)*

A._____   B._____

C._____   D._____

E._____   F._____

G._____   H._____

5. Describe the dream in detail, including its conclusion *(List every color and number that you remember)*

_____

_____

_____

_____

_____

6. Name and describe the individuals in your dream. *(If you do not know the person, state their role in your dream.)*

            Their role in the dream   Who are they to you?

A. _____   _____

B. _____   _____

C. _____   _____

D. _____   _____

7. Describe any project(s) you are currently working on?

_____

_____

_____

_____

_____

8. Briefly describe something you encountered the day before you had this dream.

_____

_____

_____

_____

_____

9. What did you have on your mind before falling asleep on the night you had this dream?

_____

_____

_____

_____

_____

Date: _____ (Enter the date of your dream.)

1. Name the dream: _____ *(This name will typically be the theme or idea of the dream)*

2. How did you feel? _____ *(Afraid, happy, lost, confused, happy, angry, etc.)*

3. Describe the theme *(What was happening, i.e., on the beach, fighting, running, at a party, Day or night, sunny, raining, etc).*

_____

_____

_____

_____

_____

4. List every symbol *(Sofa, water, pool, shoe, dirt, car, truck, dog, mom, dad, sister, etc.)*

A._____ B._____

C._____ D._____

E._____ F._____

G._____ H._____

5. Describe the dream in detail, including its conclusion *(List every color and number that you remember)*

_____

_____

_____

_____

_____

6. Name and describe the individuals in your dream. *(If you do not know the person, state their role in your dream.)*

        Their role in the dream   Who are they to you?

A. _____   _____

B. _____   _____

C. _____   _____

D. _____   _____

7. Describe any project(s) you are currently working on?

_____

_____

_____

_____

_____

8. Briefly describe something you encountered the day before you had this dream.

_____

_____

_____

_____

_____

9. What did you have on your mind before falling asleep on the night you had this dream?

_____

_____

_____

_____

_____

Date: _____ (Enter the date of your dream.)

1. Name the dream: _____ *(This name will typically be the theme or idea of the dream)*

2. How did you feel? _____ *(Afraid, happy, lost, confused, happy, angry, etc.)*

3. Describe the theme *(What was happening, i.e., on the beach, fighting, running, at a party, Day or night, sunny, raining, etc).*

_____

_____

_____

_____

_____

4. List every symbol *(Sofa, water, pool, shoe, dirt, car, truck, dog, mom, dad, sister, etc.)*

A._____   B._____

C._____   D._____

E._____   F._____

G._____   H._____

5. Describe the dream in detail, including its conclusion *(List every color and number that you remember)*

_____

_____

_____

_____

_____

6. Name and describe the individuals in your dream. *(If you do not know the person, state their role in your dream.)*

       Their role in the dream   Who are they to you?

A. _____   _____

B. _____   _____

C. _____   _____

D. _____   _____

7. Describe any project(s) you are currently working on?

_____

_____

_____

_____

_____

8. Briefly describe something you encountered the day before you had this dream.

_____

_____

_____

_____

_____

9. What did you have on your mind before falling asleep on the night you had this dream?

_____

_____

_____

_____

_____

      https://shifttothereal.com/idreammagus/

Date: _____ (Enter the date of your dream.)

1. Name the dream: _____ *(This name will typically be the theme or idea of the dream)*

2. How did you feel? _____ *(Afraid, happy, lost, confused, happy, angry, etc.)*

3. Describe the theme *(What was happening, i.e., on the beach, fighting, running, at a party, Day or night, sunny, raining, etc).*

_____

_____

_____

_____

_____

4. List every symbol *(Sofa, water, pool, shoe, dirt, car, truck, dog, mom, dad, sister, etc.)*

A._____   B._____

C._____   D._____

E._____   F._____

G._____   H._____

5. Describe the dream in detail, including its conclusion *(List every color and number that you remember)*

_____

_____

_____

_____

_____

6. Name and describe the individuals in your dream. *(If you do not know the person, state their role in your dream.)*

Their role in the dream   Who are they to you?

A. _____   _____

B. _____   _____

C. _____   _____

D. _____   _____

7. Describe any project(s) you are currently working on?

_____

_____

_____

_____

_____

8. Briefly describe something you encountered the day before you had this dream.

_____

_____

_____

_____

_____

9. What did you have on your mind before falling asleep on the night you had this dream?

_____

_____

_____

_____

https://shifttothereal.com/idreammagus/

Date: _____ (Enter the date of your dream.)

1. Name the dream: _____ *(This name will typically be the theme or idea of the dream)*

2. How did you feel? _____ *(Afraid, happy, lost, confused, happy, angry, etc.)*

3. Describe the theme *(What was happening, i.e., on the beach, fighting, running, at a party, Day or night, sunny, raining, etc).*

_____

_____

_____

_____

_____

4. List every symbol *(Sofa, water, pool, shoe, dirt, car, truck, dog, mom, dad, sister, etc.)*

   A._____   B._____

   C._____   D._____

   E._____   F._____

   G._____   H._____

5. Describe the dream in detail, including its conclusion *(List every color and number that you remember)*

_____

_____

_____

_____

_____

6. Name and describe the individuals in your dream. *(If you do not know the person, state their role in your dream.)*

       Their role in the dream   Who are they to you?

A. _____   _____

B. _____   _____

C. _____   _____

D. _____   _____

7. Describe any project(s) you are currently working on?

_____

_____

_____

_____

_____

8. Briefly describe something you encountered the day before you had this dream.

_____

_____

_____

_____

_____

9. What did you have on your mind before falling asleep on the night you had this dream?

_____

_____

_____

_____

_____

Date: _____ (Enter the date of your dream.)

1. Name the dream: _____ *(This name will typically be the theme or idea of the dream)*

2. How did you feel? _____ *(Afraid, happy, lost, confused, happy, angry, etc.)*

3. Describe the theme *(What was happening, i.e., on the beach, fighting, running, at a party, Day or night, sunny, raining, etc).*

_____

_____

_____

_____

_____

4. List every symbol *(Sofa, water, pool, shoe, dirt, car, truck, dog, mom, dad, sister, etc.)*

A._____   B._____

C._____   D._____

E._____   F._____

G._____   H._____

5. Describe the dream in detail, including its conclusion *(List every color and number that you remember)*

_____

_____

_____

_____

_____

6. Name and describe the individuals in your dream. *(If you do not know the person, state their role in your dream.)*

          Their role in the dream   Who are they to you?

A. _____   _____

B. _____   _____

C. _____   _____

D. _____   _____

7. Describe any project(s) you are currently working on?

_____

_____

_____

_____

_____

8. Briefly describe something you encountered the day before you had this dream.

_____

_____

_____

_____

_____

9. What did you have on your mind before falling asleep on the night you had this dream?

_____

_____

_____

_____

_____

                                     https://shifttothereal.com/idreammagus/

Date: _____ (Enter the date of your dream.)

1. Name the dream: _____ *(This name will typically be the theme or idea of the dream)*

2. How did you feel? _____ *(Afraid, happy, lost, confused, happy, angry, etc.)*

3. Describe the theme *(What was happening, i.e., on the beach, fighting, running, at a party, Day or night, sunny, raining, etc).*

_____

_____

_____

_____

_____

4. List every symbol *(Sofa, water, pool, shoe, dirt, car, truck, dog, mom, dad, sister, etc.)*

A._____   B._____

C._____   D._____

E._____   F._____

G._____   H._____

5. Describe the dream in detail, including its conclusion *(List every color and number that you remember)*

_____

_____

_____

_____

_____

6. Name and describe the individuals in your dream. *(If you do not know the person, state their role in your dream.)*

Their role in the dream   Who are they to you?

A. _____   _____

B. _____   _____

C. _____   _____

D. _____   _____

7. Describe any project(s) you are currently working on?

_____

_____

_____

_____

_____

8. Briefly describe something you encountered the day before you had this dream.

_____

_____

_____

_____

_____

9. What did you have on your mind before falling asleep on the night you had this dream?

_____

_____

_____

_____

                 https://shifttothereal.com/idreammagus/

Date: _____ (Enter the date of your dream.)

1. Name the dream: _____ *(This name will typically be the theme or idea of the dream)*

2. How did you feel? _____ *(Afraid, happy, lost, confused, happy, angry, etc.)*

3. Describe the theme *(What was happening, i.e., on the beach, fighting, running, at a party, Day or night, sunny, raining, etc).*

_____

_____

_____

_____

_____

4. List every symbol *(Sofa, water, pool, shoe, dirt, car, truck, dog, mom, dad, sister, etc.)*

   A._____   B._____

   C._____   D._____

   E._____   F._____

   G._____   H._____

5. Describe the dream in detail, including its conclusion *(List every color and number that you remember)*

_____

_____

_____

_____

_____

6. Name and describe the individuals in your dream. *(If you do not know the person, state their role in your dream.)*

Their role in the dream	Who are they to you?
A. _____	_____
B. _____	_____
C. _____	_____
D. _____	_____

7. Describe any project(s) you are currently working on?

_____

_____

_____

_____

_____

8. Briefly describe something you encountered the day before you had this dream.

_____

_____

_____

_____

_____

9. What did you have on your mind before falling asleep on the night you had this dream?

_____

_____

_____

_____

_____

https://shifttothereal.com/idreammagus/

Date: _____ (Enter the date of your dream.)

1. Name the dream: _____ (*This name will typically be the theme or idea of the dream*)

2. How did you feel? _____ (*Afraid, happy, lost, confused, happy, angry, etc.*)

3. Describe the theme (*What was happening, i.e., on the beach, fighting, running, at a party, Day or night, sunny, raining, etc*).

_____

_____

_____

_____

_____

4. List every symbol (*Sofa, water, pool, shoe, dirt, car, truck, dog, mom, dad, sister, etc.*)

A._____   B._____

C._____   D._____

E._____   F._____

G._____   H._____

5. Describe the dream in detail, including its conclusion (*List every color and number that you remember*)

_____

_____

_____

_____

_____

6. Name and describe the individuals in your dream. *(If you do not know the person, state their role in your dream.)*

      Their role in the dream   Who are they to you?

A. _____   _____

B. _____   _____

C. _____   _____

D. _____   _____

7. Describe any project(s) you are currently working on?

_____

_____

_____

_____

_____

8. Briefly describe something you encountered the day before you had this dream.

_____

_____

_____

_____

_____

9. What did you have on your mind before falling asleep on the night you had this dream?

_____

_____

_____

_____

_____

                                       https://shifttothereal.com/idreammagus/

Date: _____ (Enter the date of your dream.)

1. Name the dream: _____ *(This name will typically be the theme or idea of the dream)*

2. How did you feel? _____ *(Afraid, happy, lost, confused, happy, angry, etc.)*

3. Describe the theme *(What was happening, i.e., on the beach, fighting, running, at a party, Day or night, sunny, raining, etc).*

_____

_____

_____

_____

_____

4. List every symbol *(Sofa, water, pool, shoe, dirt, car, truck, dog, mom, dad, sister, etc.)*

A._____   B._____

C._____   D._____

E._____   F._____

G._____   H._____

5. Describe the dream in detail, including its conclusion *(List every color and number that you remember)*

_____

_____

_____

_____

_____

6. Name and describe the individuals in your dream. *(If you do not know the person, state their role in your dream.)*

Their role in the dream   Who are they to you?

A. _____   _____

B. _____   _____

C. _____   _____

D. _____   _____

7. Describe any project(s) you are currently working on?

_____

_____

_____

_____

_____

8. Briefly describe something you encountered the day before you had this dream.

_____

_____

_____

_____

_____

9. What did you have on your mind before falling asleep on the night you had this dream?

_____

_____

_____

_____

_____

Date: _____ (Enter the date of your dream.)

1. Name the dream: _____ *(This name will typically be the theme or idea of the dream)*

2. How did you feel? _____ *(Afraid, happy, lost, confused, happy, angry, etc.)*

3. Describe the theme *(What was happening, i.e., on the beach, fighting, running, at a party, Day or night, sunny, raining, etc).*

_____
_____
_____
_____
_____

4. List every symbol *(Sofa, water, pool, shoe, dirt, car, truck, dog, mom, dad, sister, etc.)*

A._____   B._____
C._____   D._____
E._____   F._____
G._____   H._____

5. Describe the dream in detail, including its conclusion *(List every color and number that you remember)*

_____
_____
_____
_____
_____

6. Name and describe the individuals in your dream. *(If you do not know the person, state their role in your dream.)*

        Their role in the dream   Who are they to you?

    A. _____   _____

    B. _____   _____

    C. _____   _____

    D. _____   _____

7. Describe any project(s) you are currently working on?

_____

_____

_____

_____

_____

8. Briefly describe something you encountered the day before you had this dream.

_____

_____

_____

_____

_____

9. What did you have on your mind before falling asleep on the night you had this dream?

_____

_____

_____

_____

_____

Date: _____ (Enter the date of your dream.)

1. Name the dream: _____ *(This name will typically be the theme or idea of the dream)*

2. How did you feel? _____ *(Afraid, happy, lost, confused, happy, angry, etc.)*

3. Describe the theme *(What was happening, i.e., on the beach, fighting, running, at a party, Day or night, sunny, raining, etc).*

_____

_____

_____

_____

_____

4. List every symbol *(Sofa, water, pool, shoe, dirt, car, truck, dog, mom, dad, sister, etc.)*

A._____   B._____

C._____   D._____

E._____   F._____

G._____   H._____

5. Describe the dream in detail, including its conclusion *(List every color and number that you remember)*

_____

_____

_____

_____

_____

6. Name and describe the individuals in your dream. *(If you do not know the person, state their role in your dream.)*

      Their role in the dream   Who are they to you?

A. _____   _____

B. _____   _____

C. _____   _____

D. _____   _____

7. Describe any project(s) you are currently working on?

_____

_____

_____

_____

_____

8. Briefly describe something you encountered the day before you had this dream.

_____

_____

_____

_____

_____

9. What did you have on your mind before falling asleep on the night you had this dream?

_____

_____

_____

_____

_____

https://shifttothereal.com/idreammagus/

Date: _____ (Enter the date of your dream.)

1. Name the dream: _____ *(This name will typically be the theme or idea of the dream)*

2. How did you feel? _____ *(Afraid, happy, lost, confused, happy, angry, etc.)*

3. Describe the theme *(What was happening, i.e., on the beach, fighting, running, at a party, Day or night, sunny, raining, etc).*

_____

_____

_____

_____

_____

4. List every symbol *(Sofa, water, pool, shoe, dirt, car, truck, dog, mom, dad, sister, etc.)*

A._____   B._____

C._____   D._____

E._____   F._____

G._____   H._____

5. Describe the dream in detail, including its conclusion *(List every color and number that you remember)*

_____

_____

_____

_____

_____

6. Name and describe the individuals in your dream. *(If you do not know the person, state their role in your dream.)*

          Their role in the dream   Who are they to you?

A. _____   _____

B. _____   _____

C. _____   _____

D. _____   _____

7. Describe any project(s) you are currently working on?

_____

_____

_____

_____

_____

8. Briefly describe something you encountered the day before you had this dream.

_____

_____

_____

_____

_____

9. What did you have on your mind before falling asleep on the night you had this dream?

_____

_____

_____

_____

_____

https://shifttothereal.com/idreammagus/

Date: _____ (Enter the date of your dream.)

1. Name the dream: _____ *(This name will typically be the theme or idea of the dream)*

2. How did you feel? _____ *(Afraid, happy, lost, confused, happy, angry, etc.)*

3. Describe the theme *(What was happening, i.e., on the beach, fighting, running, at a party, Day or night, sunny, raining, etc).*

_____

_____

_____

_____

_____

4. List every symbol *(Sofa, water, pool, shoe, dirt, car, truck, dog, mom, dad, sister, etc.)*

A._____   B._____

C._____   D._____

E._____   F._____

G._____   H._____

5. Describe the dream in detail, including its conclusion *(List every color and number that you remember)*

_____

_____

_____

_____

_____

6. Name and describe the individuals in your dream. *(If you do not know the person, state their role in your dream.)*

      Their role in the dream   Who are they to you?

A. _____   _____

B. _____   _____

C. _____   _____

D. _____   _____

7. Describe any project(s) you are currently working on?

_____

_____

_____

_____

_____

8. Briefly describe something you encountered the day before you had this dream.

_____

_____

_____

_____

_____

9. What did you have on your mind before falling asleep on the night you had this dream?

_____

_____

_____

_____

_____

       https://shifttothereal.com/idreammagus/

Date: _____ (Enter the date of your dream.)

1. Name the dream: _____ *(This name will typically be the theme or idea of the dream)*

2. How did you feel? _____ *(Afraid, happy, lost, confused, happy, angry, etc.)*

3. Describe the theme *(What was happening, i.e., on the beach, fighting, running, at a party, Day or night, sunny, raining, etc).*

_____

_____

_____

_____

_____

4. List every symbol *(Sofa, water, pool, shoe, dirt, car, truck, dog, mom, dad, sister, etc.)*

A._____   B._____

C._____   D._____

E._____   F._____

G._____   H._____

5. Describe the dream in detail, including its conclusion *(List every color and number that you remember)*

_____

_____

_____

_____

_____

6. Name and describe the individuals in your dream. *(If you do not know the person, state their role in your dream.)*

Their role in the dream   Who are they to you?

A. _____   _____

B. _____   _____

C. _____   _____

D. _____   _____

7. Describe any project(s) you are currently working on?

_____

_____

_____

_____

_____

8. Briefly describe something you encountered the day before you had this dream.

_____

_____

_____

_____

_____

9. What did you have on your mind before falling asleep on the night you had this dream?

_____

_____

_____

_____

_____

https://shifttothereal.com/idreammagus/

Date: _____ (Enter the date of your dream.)

1. Name the dream: _____ *(This name will typically be the theme or idea of the dream)*

2. How did you feel? _____ *(Afraid, happy, lost, confused, happy, angry, etc.)*

3. Describe the theme *(What was happening, i.e., on the beach, fighting, running, at a party, Day or night, sunny, raining, etc).*

_____

_____

_____

_____

_____

4. List every symbol *(Sofa, water, pool, shoe, dirt, car, truck, dog, mom, dad, sister, etc.)*

A._____   B._____

C._____   D._____

E._____   F._____

G._____   H._____

5. Describe the dream in detail, including its conclusion *(List every color and number that you remember)*

_____

_____

_____

_____

_____

6. Name and describe the individuals in your dream. *(If you do not know the person, state their role in your dream.)*

Their role in the dream   Who are they to you?

A. _____   _____

B. _____   _____

C. _____   _____

D. _____   _____

7. Describe any project(s) you are currently working on?

_____

_____

_____

_____

_____

8. Briefly describe something you encountered the day before you had this dream.

_____

_____

_____

_____

_____

9. What did you have on your mind before falling asleep on the night you had this dream?

_____

_____

_____

_____

_____

Date: _____ (Enter the date of your dream.)

1. Name the dream: _____ (*This name will typically be the theme or idea of the dream*)

2. How did you feel? _____ (*Afraid, happy, lost, confused, happy, angry, etc.*)

3. Describe the theme (*What was happening, i.e., on the beach, fighting, running, at a party, Day or night, sunny, raining, etc*).

_____

_____

_____

_____

_____

4. List every symbol (*Sofa, water, pool, shoe, dirt, car, truck, dog, mom, dad, sister, etc.*)

A._____   B._____

C._____   D._____

E._____   F._____

G._____   H._____

5. Describe the dream in detail, including its conclusion (*List every color and number that you remember*)

_____

_____

_____

_____

_____

6. Name and describe the individuals in your dream. *(If you do not know the person, state their role in your dream.)*

Their role in the dream   Who are they to you?

A. _____   _____

B. _____   _____

C. _____   _____

D. _____   _____

7. Describe any project(s) you are currently working on?

_____

_____

_____

_____

_____

8. Briefly describe something you encountered the day before you had this dream.

_____

_____

_____

_____

_____

9. What did you have on your mind before falling asleep on the night you had this dream?

_____

_____

_____

_____

_____

                    https://shifttothereal.com/idreammagus/

Date: _____ (Enter the date of your dream.)

1. Name the dream: _____ *(This name will typically be the theme or idea of the dream)*

2. How did you feel? _____ *(Afraid, happy, lost, confused, happy, angry, etc.)*

3. Describe the theme *(What was happening, i.e., on the beach, fighting, running, at a party, Day or night, sunny, raining, etc).*

_____

_____

_____

_____

_____

4. List every symbol *(Sofa, water, pool, shoe, dirt, car, truck, dog, mom, dad, sister, etc.)*

A._____   B._____

C._____   D._____

E._____   F._____

G._____   H._____

5. Describe the dream in detail, including its conclusion *(List every color and number that you remember)*

_____

_____

_____

_____

_____

6. Name and describe the individuals in your dream. *(If you do not know the person, state their role in your dream.)*

Their role in the dream　　　　　　　Who are they to you?

A. _____　　_____

B. _____　　_____

C. _____　　_____

D. _____　　_____

7. Describe any project(s) you are currently working on?

_____
_____
_____
_____
_____

8. Briefly describe something you encountered the day before you had this dream.

_____
_____
_____
_____
_____

9. What did you have on your mind before falling asleep on the night you had this dream?

_____
_____
_____
_____
_____

　　　　　　　　　　https://shifttothereal.com/idreammagus/

Date: _____ (Enter the date of your dream.)

1. Name the dream: _____ *(This name will typically be the theme or idea of the dream)*

2. How did you feel? _____ *(Afraid, happy, lost, confused, happy, angry, etc.)*

3. Describe the theme *(What was happening, i.e., on the beach, fighting, running, at a party, Day or night, sunny, raining, etc).*

_____

_____

_____

_____

_____

4. List every symbol *(Sofa, water, pool, shoe, dirt, car, truck, dog, mom, dad, sister, etc.)*

A._____   B._____

C._____   D._____

E._____   F._____

G._____   H._____

5. Describe the dream in detail, including its conclusion *(List every color and number that you remember)*

_____

_____

_____

_____

_____

6. Name and describe the individuals in your dream. *(If you do not know the person, state their role in your dream.)*

Their role in the dream   Who are they to you?

A. _____   _____

B. _____   _____

C. _____   _____

D. _____   _____

7. Describe any project(s) you are currently working on?

_____

_____

_____

_____

_____

8. Briefly describe something you encountered the day before you had this dream.

_____

_____

_____

_____

_____

9. What did you have on your mind before falling asleep on the night you had this dream?

_____

_____

_____

_____

_____

https://shifttothereal.com/idreammagus/

Date: _____ (Enter the date of your dream.)

1. Name the dream: _____ *(This name will typically be the theme or idea of the dream)*

2. How did you feel? _____ *(Afraid, happy, lost, confused, happy, angry, etc.)*

3. Describe the theme *(What was happening, i.e., on the beach, fighting, running, at a party, Day or night, sunny, raining, etc).*

_____

_____

_____

_____

_____

4. List every symbol *(Sofa, water, pool, shoe, dirt, car, truck, dog, mom, dad, sister, etc.)*

A._____   B._____

C._____   D._____

E._____   F._____

G._____   H._____

5. Describe the dream in detail, including its conclusion *(List every color and number that you remember)*

_____

_____

_____

_____

_____

6. Name and describe the individuals in your dream. *(If you do not know the person, state their role in your dream.)*

Their role in the dream   Who are they to you?

A. _____   _____

B. _____   _____

C. _____   _____

D. _____   _____

7. Describe any project(s) you are currently working on?

_____

_____

_____

_____

_____

8. Briefly describe something you encountered the day before you had this dream.

_____

_____

_____

_____

_____

9. What did you have on your mind before falling asleep on the night you had this dream?

_____

_____

_____

_____

_____

Date: _____ (Enter the date of your dream.)

1. Name the dream: _____ *(This name will typically be the theme or idea of the dream)*

2. How did you feel? _____ *(Afraid, happy, lost, confused, happy, angry, etc.)*

3. Describe the theme *(What was happening, i.e., on the beach, fighting, running, at a party, Day or night, sunny, raining, etc).*

_____

_____

_____

_____

_____

4. List every symbol *(Sofa, water, pool, shoe, dirt, car, truck, dog, mom, dad, sister, etc.)*

A._____   B._____

C._____   D._____

E._____   F._____

G._____   H._____

5. Describe the dream in detail, including its conclusion *(List every color and number that you remember)*

_____

_____

_____

_____

_____

6. Name and describe the individuals in your dream. *(If you do not know the person, state their role in your dream.)*

        Their role in the dream   Who are they to you?

A. _____   _____

B. _____   _____

C. _____   _____

D. _____   _____

7. Describe any project(s) you are currently working on?

_____

_____

_____

_____

8. Briefly describe something you encountered the day before you had this dream.

_____

_____

_____

_____

9. What did you have on your mind before falling asleep on the night you had this dream?

_____

_____

_____

_____

_____

            https://shifttothereal.com/idreammagus/